I'M OK, I'M PIG!

Kim Hyesoon is one of South Korea's most influential contemporary poets. She began publishing in 1979 and was one of the first few women in South Korea to be published in *Munhak kwa jisŏng* (Literature and Intellect), one of two key journals which championed the intellectual and literary movement against the US-backed military dictatorships of Park Chung Hee and Chun Doo Hwan in the 1970s and 80s. She has since won numerous literary prizes, and was the first woman to receive the coveted Midang (2006) and Kim Su-yong (1998) awards named after two major modern poets. Midang was a poet who stood for 'pure poetry' (sunsusi) while Kim Su-yong's poetry is closely associated with 'engaged poetry' (*ch'amyŏsi*) that displays historical consciousness. Kim lives in Seoul and teaches creative writing at the Seoul Institute of the Arts. She has appeared at various international festivals, including Poetry Parnassus at London's Southbank Centre, Poetry International Festival Rotterdam, Poesiefestival Berlin and Taipei Poetry Festival.

She has published three selections of her work in the US, *Mommy Must Be a Fountain of Feathers* (2008), *All the Garbage of the World, Unite!* (2011) and *Sorrowtoothpaste Mirrorcream* (2014), all with Action Books, and one with Bloodaxe Books in the UK, *I'm OK, I'm Pig!* (2014), all translated by Don Mee Choi; and most recently, Don Mee Choi's translation of *Autobiography of Death* (New Directions, USA, 2018), winner of the International Griffin Poetry Prize in 2019.

Don Mee Choi was born and grew up in Seoul and Hong Kong and now lives in Seattle. Her anthology *Anxiety of Words: Contemporary Poetry by Korean Women* was published by Zephyr Press in the US in 2006, and her own collection *The Morning News is Exciting* by Action Books in 2010. She has received a 2011 Whiting Writers Award and the 2012 Lucien Stryk Translation Prize as well as a Daesan Translation Grant, Korea Literature Translation Institute Translation Grant and an American Literary Translators Association Travel Fellowship. She has served as poet-in-residence at the Henry Art Gallery, and holds a BFA and an MFA from the California Institute for the Arts and a PhD in Modern Korean Literature and Translation from Union Institute and University.

I'M OK, I'M PIG!

KIM HYESOON

TRANSLATED BY DON MEE CHOI

BLOODAXE BOOKS

Poems copyright © Kim Hyesoon
1981, 1985, 1994, 1997, 2000, 2004, 2008, 2009, 2011, 2012
Translations © Don Mee Choi 2008, 2011, 2014

ISBN: 978 1 78037 102 3

First published 2014 by
Bloodaxe Books Ltd,
Eastburn,
South Park,
Hexham,
Northumberland NE46 1BS.

www.bloodaxebooks.com
For further information about Bloodaxe titles
please visit our website or write to
the above address for a catalogue.

The publication of this book was supported by a grant
from Literature Translation Institute of Korea.

Cover design: Neil Astley & Pamela Robertson-Pearce.

This is a digital reprint of the 2014 Bloodaxe edition.

CONTENTS

from SORROWTOOTHPASTE MIRRORCREAM

APPENDIX

ACKNOWLEDGEMENTS

I'm OK, I'm Pig! has been translated from the following titles in Korean by Kim Hyesoon:

Tto tarŭn pyŏl esŏ. Seoul: Munhak kwa chisŏng sa, 1981.
Abŏjiga seun hŏsuabi. Seoul: Munhak kwa chisŏng sa, 1985.
Na ŭi up'anisyadŭ, Sŏul. Seoul: Munhak kwa chisŏng sa, 1994.
Pulssanghan sarang kigye. Seoul: Munhak kwa chisŏng sa, 1997.
Talyŏk kongjang kongjang jangnim poseyŏ. Seoul: Munhak kwa chisŏng sa, 2000.
Han chan ŭi pulgŭn kŏul. Seoul: Munhak kwa chisŏng sa, 2004.
Tangshin ûi ch'ôt. Seoul: Munhak kwa chisông sa, 2008.
'*Maenhol inryu*' ['Manhole Humanity'] in *Chaûm kwa moûm*. Seoul, 2009.
Sûlp'ûmch'iyak kôulk'ûrim. Seoul: Munhak kwa chisông sa, 2011.
'*Twejirasô kwench'ana*' ['I'm OK, I'm Pig!'] in *Munyejungang*. Seoul, 2012.

I am most grateful to the editors, Joyelle McSweeney and Johannes Göransson, of Action Books *actionbooks.org* for granting permission to reprint the selected poems from *Mommy Must Be a Fountain of Feathers* (Action Books, 2008), *All the Garbage of the World, Unite!* (Action Books, 2011) and *Sorrowtoothpaste Mirrorcream* (Action Books, 2014). The Translator's Note was previously published in *Mommy Must Be a Fountain of Feathers*.

Kim Hyesoon's Preface was originally presented as an author's statement at Poetry Parnassus, Southbank Centre, London, in June 2012.

I would also like to thank the Literature Translation Institute of Korea and Daesan Foundation for providing translation grants.

[DMC]

PREFACE

To introduce Korean women's poetry in the space of five minutes would be as difficult as shrinking five thousand years into five minutes. The Korean male literary establishment differentiates and categorises poetry that women write as 'Women's Poetry'. However, I think that Korean women's poetry is now engaged in 'doing' poetry more than ever before. ('Doing' poetry is a term I have coined to express that women 'live' and 'do' poetry rather than write poetry, 'performing' inside and outside of poetry.)

A bear called Ung-nyô appears in the Korean creation myth called *Tang-gun*. In order to become human, the bear carries out the mission of living on only mugwort and garlic for one hundred days inside a cave. The tiger is unable to last one hundred days, but the bear is able to endure it. The bear becomes human and marries a god's son who descends from the sky and gives birth to a son. Then she disappears from the myth. In Korean mythology, women disappear after they give birth to sons. They never appear again. The ultimate goal of their existence is to give birth to sons.

However, there is one myth in which women do not disappear. This myth is about an ancestral shaman. It is a story called *The Abandoned*. A daughter is abandoned because she was born as a girl, the seventh in a row; she goes on a journey to the realm of the dead and returns to become the first shaman, a shaman whose duty is guiding the souls of the dead to a good place in the heavenly realm. In this myth a woman does not disappear after giving birth to a son. I have interpreted this narrative's symbolic meanings and researched the characteristics of poetry. In Korean culture, there exists only one area where men assume a subordinate position to women and that is at a shaman's ritual. At the ritual, the female shaman is the lead protagonist while the men merely accompany the shaman by playing instruments and doing chores such as carrying loads to set up the ritual. Perhaps this is because, at the ritual *The Abandoned*, the myth must be recited. And the women may play a bigger role because in the shamanic realm the emphasis is on performing songs and dances and being possessed by spirits.

Korean poetry has always existed in two tiers. One was metred poetry with matching numbers of syllables written by aristocratic men and the other kind was women's songs. The poems by the aristocrats were written in classical Chinese, and the men who excelled in writing poetry in the civil servant examination administered by the palace were granted a position as scholar-officials. However, women composed poems based on their daily existence, love, grief endured under their in-laws, poverty, labour, along with fantasies that arose due to oppression. These poems were sung and orally transmitted, and it was not until the 20th century that they were documented in books. The only poems by aristocratic men that I find interesting are the ones written in exile by men expelled from their government positions by the king. Their poems were written very much from a feminine position with a feminine voice. I prefer the 'voice of the expelled' in poetry by the expelled men who have been removed from power rather than poetry written by those in power.

Then those two tiers of poetry, the classical and the oral, over-lapped as one. The new genre emerged as modern poetry from the 1900s. This poetry that destroyed metre was called 'free verse' at the time. If you take a survey of Koreans' most beloved poets, the two poets that still appear at the top of the list are Kim So-wol and Han Yong-un, the poets of the 1900s. What is distinctive about their poetry is that they have chosen a female persona as their poetic persona and sing the pain of farewells in a woman's voice. This is no different from in the pre-modern period when the royal subjects sang their desire for higher government positions in a woman's voice to the king. In this woman's voice, Kim and Han expressed their grief over the injustice of the colonisation of Korea by Japan. Their poems were also very similar to the voices of the unlearned, illiterate women of the pre-modern era.

As I began writing poetry, I often felt as if my tongue were paralysed. I had no role model for poetry. The woman's voice made by Korean men, the voice that is even more feminine than a woman's, was not mine. I had no role model, especially because even pre-modern women's poetry only consisted of songs of love, farewell, and longing for the other. Even now, although not explicitly visible, many of the same aspects of the pre-modern era are still present in the poetry written by Korean men. This involves a one-to-one interaction between the subject of the poem and the poet, and from such a perspective the poet appropriates the subject as his own and creates a poem. Therefore, I thought to myself that I needed to reinvent my mother tongue. I decided to explore in my own voice the possibilities of the sensory; I decided to believe in my own feminine individuation, its secrets. For me the vast open field of the unknown and the prison existed simultaneously. Today, the young Korean women poets are developing a terrain of poetry that is combative, visceral, subversive, inventive, and ontologically feminine.

FROM

MUMMY MUST BE
A FOUNTAIN OF FEATHERS

Mummy Must Be a Fountain of Feathers

At Mummy's house, the floors are also mummy, the dust that floats around the rooms is also mummy, when you open the door of Mummy's house I'm under Mummy's feathers like an unhatched egg. All the dreams that are dreamt in Mummy's house come from Mummy's fountain, the fountain at Mummy's house is never dry. Mummy weaves dream-nests so nicely with the feathers hauled from the fountain. Breakfast at Mummy's house: teacup is feathers, coffee is feathers, and even feather-teaspoons, feather-sandwiches, a winged breakfast.

Mummy who after teaching the children steps out onto the school grounds at dusk, carrying her empty lunch box
Mummy who on a Sunday breaks the morning ice and stoops down to flog and wash a blanket cover
Mummy whose hands are cracked
My spoon that floats around in the river that has melted
Mummy who has many other chicks, besides myself, dangling below her armpits
Mummy who lost her patience one night and went out to buy an electric incubator
Uncle who lives next door and checks the sex of the chicks killed all the males and sent them to a food stall where roasted sparrows are sold
All the female chicks were sent to a boarding house
He says the female chicks will be raised to be eaten later

Beneath sleep there are stars that have not hatched yet
Stars that call me desperately
Below the stars, far below
I, another mummy, have many cold stars in my embrace

When you open Mummy's kitchen door, there's a barley field
Green barley feathers are ripening
Every drawer is full of white fuzz from chicks just pulled out from the eggs
Fat feather snowflakes are falling under the wooden floor of the living room
A feather rainbow pours out from of the attic
I hang my nighties on the rainbow
My mummy weaves dream-nests really well
but I haven't been able to incubate my sleep
because my mummy keeps telling me to wake up quickly,
and says, 'Let's eat a feather breakfast together, let's eat together'

A Sublime Kitchen

They came to eat the moon again
The women ate the moon and their bellies grew each month
They squeezed breast-milk into the moon,
added the refreshing scent of mint to the roasted moon

I caught a glimpse of her kitchen once
The secretive chirp of the cooks dressed in white
The swirling storm severing the necks of wild ducks
on hundreds of wooden chopping boards
It was a sublime kitchen

A guest with a child entered
Mummy, mummy, can I have a glass of tangy star!
She brought out a drink made of powdered rain cloud
and floated an icy star in it

I caught a glimpse of her kitchen once
The rain cloud of flour mushroomed
and all kinds of dead animals' blood flowed down the drain
the cries of countless spoons, chopsticks, fingers, toes
got sucked into the dishpan
It was a sublime kitchen

It's time to prepare a midnight meal
She cracked the moon over the frying pan
a hole as deep as a fingernail appeared on the moon
then a flock of birds crawled out from the hole
with their wings that can be fried
The flock of birds spread their black wings
across the sky as the night deepened
She roasted the wings all night

Slobbered, chewed, licked, burped, chewed and chewed, sucked, tasted,
drank, got fed nonstop, swallowed and shouted Cheers! Eat more! Hey, Over
here! One more bottle! Smacked lips, belched, gagged

Like the lips that never once closed
the buildings on both sides of the street at night
the sound of them being fed the night sky through their huge openings
Everything was sublime

The Road to Kimp'o Landfill

Cut my hair short again
I don't want to pull out
the names etched onto my hair that grows daily
As rain fell, garbage bins from the 2nd, 3rd, 4th floor
must have been turned upside down
Hair fell profusely
I kissed in a place where garbage came down like rain
I kissed where I vomited all night long
Every time I sang, vomit flew in
I turned the garbage bins upside down in my room
and had morning sickness, then had a smoke
My poetry books burned
Three hundred million babies were born
One hundred million of the young and the old died
The day I took the pills
I walked out the gate in the middle of my bath
Black plastic bags flew higher than a flock of sparrows
The discarded sewing-machine was like the head of a horse
The sound of Mother's sewing-machine
filled the holes in my body one by one
I tore off my swollen breasts and tossed them
beneath Mother's foot on the pedal
A forest gave off a foul smell, carried contagious diseases
It burned of fever during the night
A busboy at brightly lit Motel Rose
threw out millions of sperm every night
From the forest, mosquitoes swarmed
and dug into my scrawny caved-in chest
Born in the 20th century, I was on my way
to die in the 21st century

Conservatism of the Rats of Seoul

Daddy and Mummy lay us down one by one
Many of us are born – as many as Mummy's nipples
Mummy licks our eyes with her tongue softer than white bread,
licks with all her might, with darkness, darkness is cosy

Daddy who herds a fish head home also brings with him scary news
You can hear the footsteps far away, the wailing fire truck
Mummy's nipples harden
Mummy blocks the rat hole with her entire body,
our ears as well

A hairy leg enters our room. It's him. He thrashes his body around,
bam bam, shaking the house, but only the leg enters,
toenails rip Mummy's eyes, ears,
the foot in a leather shoe stomps on Mummy's skirt
Mummy isn't breathing.

He pokes around, back and forth
as many times as the minute hand of the night
You can hear the snarl all night long
He wails, pounding his head against the wall
Mummy is like a corpse and Daddy is nowhere to be seen
All night long, crushed against the house,
a hairy mouth tries to get in

By morning all is quiet – he must have left
Mummy finally gets up and breathes
Mummy bites and kills each one of us
for giving off a suspicious scent from last night's terror
She kills us then eats our intestines,
grinds her teeth against a wall
then digs out our eyeballs to eat
then there is no one
As always, only Daddy and Mummy are left
It looks as if Mummy is expecting another litter.

I'll Call Those Things My Cats

They're alive:

I'll talk about my invisible cats. They're alive. They lay two eggs every day. If they don't, they won't be able to multiply. After spring cleaning, they're in danger of extinction. They disperse with a single puff. Yet, the cats are always alive in every corner.

They're very tiny:

I don't need to give them anything to eat. Because I who am visible always leave flakes of my dead skin for them. Because my cats are tiny enough to build an apartment inside a single clot of dead skin.

They barely survive:

They fall off when brushed off, they get eaten when sucked up, they put down their tails at the smallest cough. My cats are so tiny that when they are placed under a microscope and magnified 500, 1000 times you can barely see their adorable moving lips. There's one that is fairly big. It's floating in air but always at the fringes of the dust. It trembles, afraid it might get blown away when I let out my breath, even afraid to be touched by a feather. They are powerless against the cold. In summer, I can't even open the doors. They barely survive. Poor things. Please call me mother of cats. They're so tiny that I won't be able to embrace them. It can't be helped. I need to stow them in my pores at least. A red cat peeks out between the lines of a book. Such a cute thing. The cats are everywhere. They are in the center of my brain cells. Two eggs per day. Two eggs under a blanket. Red eyes, sweet cries. My cats that wiggle behind the sofa. When I return from school, they cover themselves with the dust blanket on top of the closet – the sound of them purring, crying.

However:

These adorable things. When my life gives out, they'd eat me up in a second. When it rains, they make me drag a leather sofa outdoors. They even build houses inside my nostrils. They'd even devour my elephant. They are like the stars that can't be seen in daylight.

This Night

A rat
devours a sleeping white rabbit
Dark blood spills out of the rabbit cage
A rat devours a piglet that has fallen into a pot of porridge
(now, chunks of freshly grilled flesh inside a vagina,
babies that shiver from their first contact with air,
fattened chunks of flesh,
tasty, warm chunks that bleed when ripped into)
A rat devours the new baby in the cradle
Mummy has gone to the restaurant to wash dishes
A rat slips in and out of a freshly buried corpse

A rat that has never eaten anything that hasn't been stolen,
a rat that molds our shadows into a ball and blows into it to open our eyes,
a rat that silently burrows beneath the fungus in between the toes,
a rat that curls up its tail while eating voraciously even when it hears the rustle
     of a breath,
a rat that secretly watches us couple from behind a hidden camera,
a rat that has to grind its teeth daily, for they continue to grow,
that boasts it has seen entire eons of evolution

In between the tiny blood vessels inside our glaring exterior,
inside the dark slippery intestines beneath the soft skin,
in between the wiggling toes under the creaking floor,
inside the skull where the echoing footsteps of rain and wind hide out,
inside that dark place of my body that not even a single ray of light can penetrate,
inside that belly of the body of death tucked inside my body for years,
a rat grinds its teeth to devour the fingers

this night

Rat

Enter the inside of the sunny morning, and it seems as if the scream can always be heard. It's so loud that it's inaudible to us. The scream let out by last night's darkness. This morning the whitish scream suddenly disperses then gathers in the air – *ah, ah, ah, ah!* Do people know how much it hurts the darkness when you turn on the light in the middle of the night? So I can't turn on the light even when the night arrives. The day of the first snowfall, I took an x-ray of my body. Then I asked everyone I met: Have you ever turned on the light inside your intestine? The darkness with a fluid mass moving through it endlessly – is this my essence? When the light is switched on inside my darkness, I buzz like a beetle pinned down, *bung, bung, bung, bung*, and shake my head wildly, my muzzle holding onto a black string. Struck by the light, I regress, in a flash, from a reptile to a beetle turned upside down. My dignity is the darkness inside. Was it hiding inside the darkness? Lights on – my underground prison, my beloved black being trembles in it. The damaged walls of my room quiver from the car lights coming in through the windows. Thousands of rays of light poke at me – my dark, crouched face. The day of the first snow, the snow was nowhere to be seen. The houses with lit windows. How painful the light must be for the night.

A Hen

Rain hammers away at the keyboard till it's all bloody red mud splatters trees
fall and the chickens tremble inside the water-filled coop she hammers away
till the keyboard is bloodied she hammers away so hard that a crimson flower
of flesh blooms on top of her skull the crown flutters like a flag, her heart
placed on top of her head the lit window screams because the light in the
room was turned off at one point her typewriter-teeth endlessly collect the
feed onto the paper she lowers her head, feels her forehead three women left
home today they left the coop crying you all know where they have been
taken she spreads her ten fingers and clutches her desk, types the tears one at
a time night arrives and the rain lets up her beloved's leather shoes drop
outside the window and she lays an egg while hammering away at the keyboard
the conveyer belt swiftly takes away her egg she mustn't go outside today her
body, the book of pain, has barely made it through a page of flesh, bleeding,
but the calendar she pecks out daily is still on the same page why is she
making a calendar that no one looks at? her eyes want to sleep, so they close
slowly from the bottom to the top outside the window, the rain, as if it had
been lying in wait, begins to hammer away at the keyboard blood splatters on
the window her eyes flash open and her heart, a loop of painful blood vessels,
flinches and bleeds on top of her head the crown turns crimson once again

The Saints – Mr and Mrs Janitor

They are rummaging through the corpses. Those who ignite and hold the torchlights. Outside our sleep, the roads are wet from the rain, and they tear off our nametags. The torn-off nametags quickly pile up into a heap. Eyeglasses pile up with eyeglasses. Suitcases with suitcases. Shinbones with shinbones. Babies with babies who are thrown out into the future far, far away. The years that I've lived heap up, and on the side of the road a trial slowly goes on inside a green metal booth. A blazing bonfire. One of the janitors throws my book towards the fire. It flares up every time the book lands, and the leather shoes from which my feet have slipped, that used to roam around like a pair of fat married rats, give off a stench as they burn. The janitors who wear masks like the KKK, with a glowing cross on their backs, press down on my three meals with their feet. They sweep up the intestines that burst and spill out. My naked body folded tightly gets pressed down once again by their feet before heading for the gas chamber. The pressed corpses are placed in sacks then loaded onto a truck. Behind the door of my sleep, the Auschwitz of Seoul unfolds all night long. Teeth with teeth, fingernails with fingernails. The stench circles the same spot unable to disperse during the rainy night. The janitors finish up the job of sorting, load the corpses dripping with gravy, and take off down the road next to an apartment building. They need to hurry, for once again, today, the crematories are full and the grounds are already filled with corpses. The collapsed pink department store – we wept and clapped hysterically when the janitors like aged babies made it out alive from under the heap of 500 dead bodies. The saints, Mr and Mrs Janitor, who will live forever, tie me up – I who will utter 'O Time' – and exit the sleeping city. The torn black sacks flutter like an elegy. Whose skull is this? A head with closed eyes falls from the truck and gets crushed again inside my dream.

When the Plug Gets Unplugged

Chickens die first inside the plastic greenhouse. Eggs rot on the conveyor belt. Rotten pigs packed in the refrigerated trucks are delivered to all the butcher shops, the dead float up in the aquarium. The farmer's market at Karakdong decays and the filth swells up inside my body and

you and I begin to rot in the open. I can't leave the lights on for you any longer. We can no longer look each other in the face. You are completely cut off from me. Our skin melts, so anyone can look into anyone's intestines. Toilets also overflow in dreams. Nothing goes down no matter how many times you flush. Even the candles give off a stench. If you have a flame thrower or a tidal wave,

please send it to me. Belgrade fell into darkness from the bombs that emitted black smoke. As the fighter jet dropped the bombs, the bombs exploded over the target and released black powder. The charged powder stuck to the power lines, caused a short circuit, burnt the lines, and disabled the power towers. NATO troops paralysed the Yugoslav troops' information network, scrambling their computer system. Inside a dim room where the computers sit not saying anything

crazy people increase in numbers. Birds shudder and fall off and flowers begin to eat worms. Furthermore, there are flowers that bite people. Here, below my feet, is the interior of the world. The dead chickens on the mud floor are strewn like mountains. Now, I throw salt at you – what little is left of you – inside my heart. Instead, the microbes that have remained dormant within my skin enlarge. They become as big as ants, then hedgehogs, and this morning they became as big as dogs.

The dogs bite off our remaining days and roam. Rotten nipples of the world's mothers drop like beans. Flies swarm what's left of the torn bodies. That is how pervasive darkness is. Ghosts eat food that has gone bad and stagger off as if being tied up and pulled away on someone's rope. Now you and I are merely shadows. Above the shadows, inside the sunlight, our silhouettes melt. We're alive, but our brains contain only lumps of rice that have gone sour. With all the forms destroyed, only the meanings bubble up from the honey bucket and fall, then bubble up again. Please send me a flame thrower or a tidal wave as soon as possible.

Seoul, My Oasis

The house moves in. The house that can't be scooped out. The house across from us is rushing in, reaching our family room. The whole family is trying to restrain the house, but it has already swallowed up half of our house. The walls around the yard have disappeared and the car is trapped in the house. Move the car! The man from the house across the street slaps my face. The houses pile up like stairs and the stairs pile up inside the houses, the houses endlessly flow in. The puppy that snuck outside was crushed to death by the houses moving in. It has been a while since the alley where dogs can shit has disappeared. The corpses that have just breathed their last are suffocated again by the houses rushing in and expire once again. There is no empty land to lay down the coffins. There is no room for shadows in my yard. Stand and hold up the walls. Daddy's arms are swollen from holding up the walls. Mummy easily gets depressed and daddy beats mummy who sleeps all the time. However, mummy is caught between the houses and can't run away, so she gives birth to her young. Inside a room that is dark even though the window is hung in the air, my younger siblings pucker their lips waiting for food like young swallows. My siblings who get hungrier as they eat. On ancestor day, the ghosts can't breath, can't breath, so they can't eat either and return to their underground apartments. From there the cries flow out daily, daddies make folksy crafts that no one buys, and the sad music of the dead from the other world, the depths of the underground, where corpses collect can be heard every night. Bricks pile up daily outside the window and concrete pours into my mouth. The houses move in like the sand of the Sahara that tumbles into an oasis. The houses that build houses inside my nostrils, earlobes, and hair. When the wind blows, the overgrown roofs, the wavering pillars, the pulsating windows, the antennas that transmit cries, and there is no one in Seoul – only neatly piled up houses.

Asura, Yi Je-ha, Spring

In the middle of the night, a car speeds along a windy road. The people from
the North who came over in a submarine – they've killed each other. This time
a tunnel appears after the car goes down ninety-nine windy roads where the
dead bodies are scattered. The car enters the tunnel. The end of the tunnel is
not visible. The tunnel is dark. All the lights inside the tunnel are broken. I
want to get out of the tunnel, the car shouts. The tunnel is round. The tunnel
spins by itself. It's cold inside the tunnel. The car screams alone. An echo
bounces back each time the tunnel spins around. Echo, echo. A swirling echo.
It's damp in here. The car screams non-stop into the dampness. Even the car's
headlights are turning. Dozens of them from the North had to kill themselves
just because their submarine landed secretly in the South. Was the mountain
this huge and heavy? It's as if the car had passed several underground
mountain ranges. Right turn, left turn, right turn again. No one is following.
Hold your breath. Curve, curve, cup... there's nothing. At once the tunnel
explodes black like a black aquarium. There is no mountain or tunnel. There
is no road or sky. My entire body wants to shoot out of my face. I want to lie
down. A scream floats up from somewhere inside my body. The car spins
inside the tunnel within the body. Something leaps out from the inside of my
body like the way a frog flattened in an illustration swells up into life. That
thing, that slippery green light, that thing with thousands of heads, that thing
with ten thousand fingers closes my eyes and ears and licks my face with its
tongue. With its other tongue it licks my hair. It licks my chest. Its several
hundred hands strangle me as it plants a heavy kiss on my eyelids. I let go of
the steering wheel and clutch onto that thing. I bite into it. The car runs
freely all by itself. If you look in from the outside, someone is fighting with
an Asura. The Asura is not visible, but it's slippery. That invisible thing
overpowers someone. Someone who is neither a man nor a woman grabs that
thing and throws it out the window. That thing shatters into dirty green. The
dirty green spreads to the east, west, south, and north. The car has left the
tunnel, but there is no car on the road. Suddenly, it's spring!

NOTES: A ghost that enjoys fighting, Asura is a familiar figure in Buddhism. Yi Je-ha is a
contemporary South Korean writer. In September 1996, a North Korean submarine broke
down and landed on the east coast of South Korea. Eleven North Koreans were found dead
on a nearby mountain. They had shot each other in an apparent suicide pact. In all 24 North
Koreans were killed or found dead during the massive hunt carried out by South Korean
troops. North Korea claimed that the submarine accidentally drifted into South Korea's
waters, but South Korea maintained that the submarine was on a spying mission. [DMC]

The Movie Our Descendants Most Hated

We are always caught between June 25 and May 18
In between them music spins and goes insane as it spins
Inside my head, a prison riot
Electrical lines are clanging away
a searchlight flickers from the surveillance tower
That *vocal* is definitely out of his mind
Out of the blue
my students take me by the hand and pull me towards them, saying,
'Teacher, see how we are *banging* our heads'
Dust falls like the last days of Pompeii
it glitters then crumbles, it wavers then shatters and swirls
We face each other and release black balloons
we recite our names chanting, Let's not part from one another
The black balloons burst in air, leaflets fall out
Every time the vocal screams,
'I only exist inside your head
I'll get to see the hell within you for sure'
I say, 'No, no'
Entire lifetimes flicker with a lamp in each hand
but all the days younger than today muss up my hair
Can't breathe unless I scream with all my might
It's our turn when the *vocal* falls silent
Inside that music,
the circle of June 25 and May 18 narrows as it repeats itself
that place where we'll vanish after we go round and round is the inside of my
    head
The prison heaves like a cat in a black garbage bag tied with the night's hair
A helicopter takes off and people in uniform circle the prison
We've missed the emergency exit

NOTES: Koreans use the English word 'vocal' to refer to a singer in a band. The Korean
War began on June 25, 1950. Over four million people died in the war, which ended in
1953. North and South Korea still remain divided. May 18 refers to the Kwangju uprising
of 1980 when, with the tacit consent of the US, South Korean troops massacred several
hundred civilians. The pro-democratic movement was protesting political and economic
oppression under South Korea's military dictatorships. [DMC]

Father Is Heavy, What Do I Do?

Child,
a hundred-year-old fox devours one hundred humans
and becomes a woman.
I, a woman poet, devour one hundred fathers
and become a father.
(How repulsive! Now I will have a five o'clock shadow)
I devour one hundred fathers,
and as I look around,
lifting high the knife of a narrative
sharpened by the teeth of fibs about the fathers.
Look at you, entering between the sentences, riding a donkey.
Eloi, Eloi!

Father returns from a field, where you are planted, after treating it with pesticide.
Father chops off your arm and makes a wooden platform.
Father chops off your lower trunk and sends it to a lumberyard.
Father's hands are vicious blades.
Father has acres to pace, wearing his big leather shoes.
Father is startled when I say to him, 'Father, play with me!'
I shout, 'I don't want to become a father!'
But Father became a father because he'd killed father, his father's father.
Steel-curtain-father, black-ink-father, machine-heart-father.
Father has to bring his hands together sharpened like blades
in order to pierce my heart – that kind of father.
Child, I've become such a repulsive Father.

A Hundred-Year-Old-Fox

I came to find a peach in this life
I came to find the red stain, the stain from the bite
of the peach you spat out as you departed
They say you are sick in the world of ghosts
but I am in the frozen mountain valley of a snowy night
I think I must have been possessed by the field of snow
Where am I?
They say when you circle the entire field, red baby
becomes white grandma and white grandma becomes red baby
Peach blossom flurries, flurries of snow
fall and keeps falling again
and yet the endless white paper
The footprints of my life are erased as soon as they are made
The bloodshot eye opens somewhere deep in the ground
The hot thing that popped out from my womb
The pencil breaks, I have a lot of homework
But where is it really?
It seems as if the peach scent is coming from somewhere

A White Horse

What happens if a white horse suddenly enters my room? what if the horse
completely fills my entire room? what if the horse shoves me into its huge
eyeball and keeps me in there? a shiny train enters the horse and dark people
get off the train the sun fades and as the door of the deserted house opens she
who is dark grabs onto her torn blouse and runs out and the stars amass
around her ankles wait a second then she goes into the empty house and
drinks pesticide then runs out and as she runs she tries to vomit out the horse
by holding onto a tree but the horse never leaves once it has entered she's
unable to cry she can only hiccup as the horse's mane may be tickling her
throat what if the horse never leaves her body? what if the white horse grabs
onto the paths engraved inside the body all night long and won't let a single
train enter? what do I do? do I go and ask the woman who endures a horse
inside her unable to say a single word because the pesticide has destroyed her
vocal cords? here is my room but I can't enter or leave a horse aimlessly
stands in the room

The Way To Melodrama 4

white day white night

White snow. White rabbit. White night because white snow fell overnight. White rabbit stares at white steel-barred window. White gown. White sheet. White wrist. White hat. White skirt. White legs turning. White sandal. Gave birth to a white baby because of white snow. White rice that you eat while holding a white umbrella. I ate it--a white pill that makes white blood. White God inside white snow rises as high as the window. There is a white secret inside white snow. White blanket. White sweat. White skin of baby Jesus. The white wall is too high. White lips. White nose. There are too many white rats in white milk. White breath, can't breathe. There is no road because white snow keeps coming down. White devil. White hell. It's too far. White yawn. White sleep. Please untie white bandages. White writing on white paper. I will erase my white poem. Oblivious innocence of White God, open my blood's path outwards.

> It's remarkable.
> Every morning I open my white eyelids,
> squeeze out white toothpaste,
> and shove it against my white teeth as I
> tear open a white tent and walk out the door.

White shovel inside white snow. One white house. White window. White lamp inside a white curtain. White grandfather, please eat. White bread sent from God. White butterfly. Butterfly. Butterfly. Butterfly. Mother, please look at the white butterfly. My god, how can this be? How many days has it been? White mother. White cough. White sigh. White breasts. White powdery snow slides in back of white ears and falls softly softly on top of a desk. White snow is falling. Young white woman's white smile. White birds land and pile up one by one. Closed eyes of the birds. White bird is pressing me down. It's too heavy. Please remove the blanket. Jellyfish multiply inside the sea. Sea becomes firm like jelly. White sea. Sea crumbles like white powder. White rabbit on top of white sand. White wrist. White needle.

> White snow fills up
> the white snow wall fills up
> but I keep pushing the white wall high high up into the air
> Where is the end of my old civilisation?
> Hell of tenderness
> A white ant that fell into white sugar hell
> White sugar melts
> White sugar hell binds the white ant like honey
> Can't breathe

29

Why Can't We

leave Buddha alone? We make Buddha ride an elephant like the way a village
boy rides on a man's shoulder, and we let the Buddha run and play, then
make him cry, and we make him couple blissfully with a buttery woman and
call it Tantra, but then we make him smile by himself in emptiness, make
him sit, lie down, make him be born from the waist, then teach him how to
walk right away, and we question him when he lies down to sleep You said
this and that didn't you? and we braid his fingers, cut off his nose and
swallow it down with water, then dress him in gold, but then we cut his
throat and sell his head at a store in Insadong, and we lock him up inside a
cave on top of a mountain, and as if that weren't enough we keep him inside
a rock, starve him, paint his skin gold so that he can't even breathe, have him
stand faraway on top of a mountain and caress him slowly as we approach
him by boat, and beneath his feet we beg him to beat us up. Why can't we
leave him alone? We build a house on a cliff overlooking a blue river and lock
him up and a bunch of us go together to gawk at him. We pummel him,
crush him, and push him over, then we come home and write a letter of
apology in blood from our pierced fingers, and we pull his teeth and divide
them up into numerous pouches and give them out to the whole world, and
why do we go near him and bow on our knees till they are raw and look once
into his eyes then return home with our downcast faces?

Grief

God raised cows on a ranch in the sea
The cows fattened leisurely eating grass
There were no herders, no fences
We couldn't see even with our eyes open
but every cow's head was branded with God's seal
God played a flute when night came
All the blue cows were gathered
God scoffed at all the cows

I stole one of the cows and
gave it to a Mongolian who
with one hand kept the lamb's mouth shut
and with another made a hole in its heart
He said, this cow belongs to the sea
It has no fur, no flesh. We don't eat anything from the sea
The cow belongs to him – his body made entirely of tears
The lamb he caught was skinned
without a single drop of blood or a scream

This time I had no choice but
to eat the blue cow by myself
My body became covered in blue mold
I couldn't feel the cold and roamed the streets in sub-zero weather
Except for the salt crystals falling from one of my eyes
The sea grabbed my ears every where I went
and rippled all day
I couldn't sleep at all

Water Spider's House

Naturally, rain fell from the sky
(However, she didn't get wet)
She took a bus to her house
(She didn't have a home)
All the passengers on the bus had a home
(However she didn't have a home)
The windows of the bus are segmented like a cartoon
(The cliffs with numbers attached to them honked and sped up)
The bus soon arrived at the terminal
(However, in truth the bus didn't have a terminal)
She stopped in front of her house
(Her house shook as though it were hanging from a swing)
She quietly rolled up her face then tucked it between her legs
(She didn't have legs)
Was her house hiding inside her body?
(The house grabbed her by the throat)
Everywhere I step is my home – did she believe this?
(There was no floor to spread a blanket out on in her house)
Was the road a home for her?
(She just stood there holding her house)
Ripples continuously spread above the roof
(Her house didn't have a roof)
Her house flowed down from the crown of her head like blood
(Who pulled out the house?)
Doors fell
(However, in truth her house didn't have any doors)
The doors flowed downstream
(The river was crammed with her doors)
Her house that quietly crumbles into the river
(Where have you been your whole life?)
A lifetime of rain from the sky
(However she didn't get wet)
Her house that she can't even live in
(Her house that is draped with her eyes)

Seoul's Dinner

Flowers enter. The flowers with puckered lips. The flowers that fill the back of a truck suck on the wall of the tunnel. The tunnel reddens momentarily. She plucks off the new leaves and shoves them into her mouth. Angelica shoots drop from angelica trees and fall into the dish of seasoned soy sauce. A truckload of angelica enters. Angelica shoots turn the mouth of Seoul green. Flatfish enter. A thousand flatfish packed in ice enter, swooning. A truckload of the East Sea enters. Pigs enter. The pigs oink and suck on Seoul's lips. She dips the meat from the pig's neck in pickled shrimp and eats. Her squirming throat is omnivorous. Mudfish pour in like a muddy stream. The Taebaek range is shredded and enters, squirming. The fields of the higher ranges of Mount Sŏrak enter, salted. Radishes revealing only the top half of their white bottoms are neatly stacked onto a truck. Trucks with their lights on enter. They line up and enter in between the teeth. When the trucks leave the tunnel, Seoul's blue stomach acid embraces them. Some of the trucks with big eyes try to make their way through the sea of acid, but the darkness inside Seoul's intestine is dense. Greens in sacks enter. Thousands of chickens with reddened crowns follow thousands of eggs just laid today and enter. Bulls as big as elephants their eyes fiercely opened enter. Bulls charge the path inside the body of someone who lives in Seoul. Tonight she drinks too much soju. The tunnel where the liquor is poured is long and dark. White milk that could overflow Lake Soyang pours out of the tunnel into the night's intestine. The plains of Honam enter. But in the opposite lane, trucks loaded with waste water purifiers have lined up in single file. Having left the party, I begin to vomit as soon as I step outside. Seoul eats and shits through the same door. My body curls up like a worm. It seems that every few days a big hand descends from the sky to roll out cloud-like toilet paper and wipe the opening of Seoul, which is simultaneously a mouth and an anus. Tonight, fat flakes fall as the last truck leaves the tunnel. I let the snow collect, then shove it into my mouth.

A Hole

A hole walked in just as I was wiping off my makeup
I looked at the hole as I sat on the sofa and took off my stockings
The hole was about one metre and sixty centimetres wide
I hear the hole makes good steamed rice
and on some days babies pop out from it
However the hole isn't certain whether someone is spitting into it or not
and even when a black cloud sits leaning against its thighs for decades
it doesn't care
A fool, like a hell that keeps on walking
I poured left-over seaweed soup into the hole
Really the hole is nothing an idiot but it's deep
When I took out my wisdom tooth a one-metre-and-sixty-centimetres-wide hole
opened up
However the problem is that a hole falls into the hole endlessly whenever it can
Where's the hole's end?
The hole remains a hole even if the water from all the ponds of the world is
poured into it
Do people know that the hole puts on makeup?
That it cries when it is hit by lightening?
That a red tongue that detests the hole hides inside the hole's mouth and kneads
an ohohoh sound?
The hole intensifies when it stays in bed too long
In other words the hole becomes deeper and deeper
When I get up in the morning I see a mark on my pillow
from the tears of the hole

The Cultural Revolution Inside My Dream

The main ingredient of my social standing is reaction
Night after night I go to school to write the confession of my crime
My lover, a photon, is a Red Guard who enjoys digging
The photon has many lovers, dispatched from the sun
to the inside of my dream, maybe it's a prison guard or a murderer
After copulation, it devours its lovers
Even though I confess my crimes day by day, there are always more left

I'm so exhausted today. My eyelids feel like a ton of bricks and my ears pull
down the shutters, the photon that has been pacing outside my dream knocks
on the door. Photon, please, I'm worn out today. After a long day of roaming
inside sunlight and being crushed by the photon as flat as a screen, the photon
inserts a confessional program into my body. I'm too sick today, just forgive
me, please. The photon makes a hole in my body, goes deep into my flesh
with a spade and bangs on my bones with its beak. The photon that is as
bright as a star. The photon that flickers on the TV screen after the broadcast
has ended. The photon calls my name, gets furious at me, encircles me, blabs
to its heart's content. The confession that I write again and again. The photon
enjoys itself, uses the waterfall of my blood for its mirror. I've written so many
confessions that I don't know what's what. Things are mixed up to the point
that my father is transformed into my child. How wonderful it would be to
sleep even one night outside the house of the photon. A few decades ago, when
I used to work for a publisher, I went to the city hall to get the manuscripts
inspected. Mr Military Officers with black ink would hand me back the pages
after smearing ink all over them. Sometimes the entire manuscript was
blackened except for the title. Where did all the blackened Mr Officers go?

The photon plays all night, using the inside
of my body as a screen, and today it has made
my dead grandmother much younger than me
Grandmother took out a charcoal briquette from the furnace
then replaced it with the full moon on fire
Inside the room, Mother lay down after giving birth and cried
There were people inside each teardrop, so I asked,
'Who are you?' They replied that they were Mother's spirits
But when I looked closely into the teardrops, the people were all me
Inside the closed school, I was sitting on all the benches
reading aloud from my confessions, and the voice informed me that
Grandmother grows up and becomes Mother
and Mother grows and becomes me

There are so many of me that I feel like I'm going to die
Every night I collectively
go to school to write confessions
go to the photon to get censored

Spring Rain

I missed my stop from thinking of you
Rain fell as I pressed the bell stop, Please let me off
People in the street walked slantwise
Their screams as I jumped into the rain
The birds that talk inside the throats of the people running peeked out
Each of them shouted, I don't want to live inside someone else
A man followed a woman and a woman followed a woman and
a woman ran, following the previous man
Mr who got off the same bus behind me followed, calling me, Sis, Sis
The handkerchief in front of his chest flapped like a flower with a broken stem
The sky with a damaged immune system coughed away
Dark spots below the thighs were spreading
All the clock hands attached to the rooftops slanted to the right
A previously frozen lump of clay began to melt
Ugly faces fell and splashed down onto the ground and rolled about
The birds that live inside other people's bodies flew up all together
They spat as they kept shouting
My head that used to think about you spreads to the rest of the street

A Question Mark

Someone is taking out
a question from a question mark.
Question that flew like a chicken feather,
question that gave its body to the wind,
question that stripped naked,
question that painted the entire body,
question with a hidden face,
question that cried.

Question's tears. Tears' flood. Question's knee. Pull up the knee, question.
Turn over, question. Good, question. Bark like a dog, question. Question,
open your mouth. Question's saliva. Saliva's flood. Question, careful with the
knee. Question that bites off a question. Don't sleep, question. Sing, question.
Flap around like the wind, question. Comma, enter here. Block the question.
Don't let it out, comma. Question, question, back in place. Singing question.
Question that left a period. Question that is lonely from one remaining
question. Question made up of a tail. Question with a tail up after the rain.
Oh poor question that bit its lip while being blown about.

A period that lost a tail
cries silently.
Now someone draws near a period
and tries to shove in
a fallen question.

To Patients with Contagious Diseases

breathlessly

Run, holding, only, your, lit, ten, ta, cle, blue, and, cold. Go, run. Give, your, bodies, to, mag, gots, that, feed, on, bodies, sell, frenzied, your, legs, to, people, who, come, to, buy, legs, and, shout your bids. Vomit, excrete, dribble, give, away, everything, every thing. Pull out and show, your, wick. Run. Sick, Body, when, someone, calls, you, shout back, I'm alivealive. Don't, arrive, just, de, part. Run, so, that, the, needles, can, slip out, white, beds, can, crumble, bloody shit, can, splatter, and, dead things, and, stench, can, fly, high up, in, the, sky. Life, leavesthenreturns, departsthenarrives, and, the, sick, body, burns, up, then, takes, on, life, and, runs, out, again! Look, over there, there. Happiness, painted, in oil, is, inside, a frame, and, now, sa. ccha. rine. Of happiness, flows, like. a. ri. ver. Into, my, blood. If someone, asks, Is anyone alive? Break, your, head, open, and, show, your, ten, ta, cle.
Sick
      bodies
           that
              keep
                  talking
                      in
                          their
                              sleep
                                  !

They Beat Me Up

'I like A,' I said.

Then B ran towards me and hit me.

When I said, 'B hit me because I said I liked A,' C ran towards me and beat me.

When I said, 'B hit me because I said I liked A, and because I said B hit me C hit me,' A ran towards me and beat me.

When I said, 'B hit me because I said I liked A; because I said B hit me C hit me; and A hit me because I said C hit me,' A, B, C, all ran toward me and beat me.

Now I had no choice but to get beaten up and pant, 'They got me, they got me.'

And I couldn't even remember who it was that I liked.

Face

There is another you inside you

The you inside you pulls you tight into the inside, so your fingernails curl inward and your outer ears swirl into the inside of your body you would probably leave this life the moment the you inside you lets go of the hand that grabs you

Your face stays frozen in motion as the you inside you pulls you hard at times, that face leans towards mine outside of you and I can feel the you inside you looking at me from the inside of your eyes; but the you inside you has never once let go of the hand that grabs you as always you are pulled tight now your face has deep creases from the strain

The you inside you is so strong that the I inside me is about to get dragged into your inside

Now you are drinking a glass of red wine, holding a piece of cheese in your hand

The I inside me thinks about the fact that the cheese is made of milk then worries about which cow inside the cow has spurted out the milk

Even if you are far away, another you inside you is here I can't return or avoid the you inside you

Maybe I am the hostage of an absent being

I will certainly stay alive while the I inside me clutches onto me; furthermore, I want to deliver the cheese made of me inside me to your table every morning

An Old Fridge

I'm desperately holding back the urge – my feet want to reach you before me. I'm desperately holding back the urge – my lips want to reach you before me. I've held back like this for decades. It's strange when I think about it. It seems that I've been holding back since I got a fridge of my own. Anyhow, I've been thinking. My head is completely filled with ice. Anyone who touches my cold feet faints. The lips of those who enter my heart freeze. Therefore, I won't budge from here. I won't hold out my arms to anyone. I think to myself that I won't forget any of this. Because I'm desperately holding back like this not a single leaf drops in my room, not a single bird can take off from the ground. I'll hold out with my fingers plugged into the 220-volt outlet even if the wind blows. The frozen painting of a landscape, how beautiful! The ice princess of the ice world inside the landscape, how pure! I won't worry even if blood drips down her thighs because it will freeze right away. It's hot outside and cold inside. It's so cold that it's boiling. When the door opens, I'm so startled that I turn on the light, frozen intestines hang from the winter landscape. The power has been out for several days because of the typhoon, and for decades I've been acting as if nothing's wrong till the inside of my body begins rotting away.

Boiling

You fly deep into the night sky
I can detect your heat while I sleep
A cruise missile has launched!
The heat of explosion far above the sky!
Soon the water in a pot boils
I can't sleep, so I might as well have a cup of coffee
I almost dip my hand into the boiling water
for the boiling water looks so cold
Instead I dip my head inside the pot and say something
Are thousands of layers of ear membranes boiling?
Or are they a metaphor for birth and death?
Thousands of Morse codes undulate in the evaporating boiling water
It is like the Mass in a cathedral
The condor shoots straight up against the harsh air streams
slowly circles, then rapidly descends
and looks down distantly at the boiling water
Maybe someone has hidden a helicopter in the forest
From faraway the sound of the trees boiling
The thousands of electrical wires are pinned to the body's interior
begin to emit electricity to the inside, inside
this is not just a feeling but an ultrasound, a hydro-current
my inside can get electrocuted when I place my hand in it
this time I begin to boil like an electric pot
this isn't love but an electricity detector, a missile
Hear a boiling sound from the ear
Swish, swish, I escape from my body
All the water evaporates

Silent Night, Holy Night

It was already too late when I dug into the grave, the corpse that had already
been devoured by rats showed up and my back ached. The organs inside the
back ached, the organs shrieked and rattled the bones, and a hired man said
that, if I wanted to find a fat rat, I needed to turn this cemetery inside out. It
was fashionable to have babies in your forties and, strangely, azaleas blossomed
from a rose bush and acacias smelled like lilacs. Pyŏkje Cremation was in great
demand and mismatched legs kept arriving and piling into the coffin and in
one coffin there was only the hand of a woman. The beautician was dead on
her feet. I flew to Spain to watch flamenco and watched it again as I rotated
once, for 12 beats, rotated twice, for 24, and repeated, 'O Time, be gone, be
gone,' and from where I was sitting I wished for many lifetimes to pass. My
lover would only talk to me in code and a Japanese critic was up in arms,
'That's just how I am. What's your story?' Even though I was told that
scorpions were submerged inside the rain-soaked mud, I rooted in it and
smeared it on my face. The president of each country signed an exchange so
that the corpses of dead husbands could be returned as Christmas gifts from
the war-torn country and my students shouted towards the screen 'Nature!' But
my fellow poets ripped the screen and shouted towards the darkness, 'Here is
nature,' and we carefully considered whether the remaining enemy of Father
was also our enemy. While we were deep in thought, only the women factory
workers who weren't hooked up to the internet bought fiction. Then one day,
I raise the lid of the manhole that empties into the canal. The rats that open
their eyes only in the dark, their eyes that have turned the colour of sewage,
their teeth that have become sharp as picks from digging around with their
black eyes open. The rats startled by the light trickling in run away with their
hairless litters that have just opened their eyes in their mother's embrace and

FROM

**ALL THE GARBAGE
OF THE WORLD, UNITE!**

Manhole Humanity

O

Goodness, I didn't know there were such repulsive holes!

My hairy holes!
Creases of my stomach
Hair-like cilia in my nostrils
Finger-like villi in my small intestine
Pubic hair of love
Hair sprouts up inside the holes and ripples like water plants.
Holes are neatneatly piled inside a steaming stomach.
The wet and most poisonous snakes in the world pant.
Fill us up! Fill us up with the outside!
Delicious outside!
When hair whines like the fingers that reach out towards the refugee-aid bread truck someone picks up a brass instrument and wails at the sky praising the blueness.
Holes of the world, open up your lids and howl!

O

Bile travels up the esophagus and collects in my mouth. My oesophagus feels as if it's burning. The drain regurgitates. It's potent. It's as if ceiling and floor are stuck together. Right now I'm being thrashed about by a whip made of horizontal lines. In my dream someone comes into my room to surf.

In my dream I burn like a charcoal briquette, a wick placed down in my neck. In the next dream, I become a gas in the dream world of gases. I hear wind in my ears.

I dream of my holes falling onto a cement floor. I clean them up with a plastic brush.

A tap leaks. Water starts to collect in the basement. My pillow floats above the basement.

Look over this way! As I open my eyes, the doctor pokes my tear glands with a long needle. Tears collect in my mouth. They're salty. I stare at the ocean inside me.

Nerve holes of a neck become constricted and put pressure on the entire nerve tree. A tranquilliser is injected directly into the holes. It is given six times a day. The piano keeps shut its gum that is about to spew out blood.

My right shoulder hurts, but the doctor inserts a needle in my left toe. With a stick, the doctor explains the swirls of my holes and the structure of my spirals. Someone sticks his head outside my manhole and looks out. Someone screams from my throat.

My body covered with holes wants to escape leaving the holes behind.

Nausea comes up the hole. As I take off my skin, the pipes holed in my body leak.

A lit stethoscope moves through the pipe. A night bus dashes along the endless roads inside my body. The night bus flickers like pain.

O

Hole, the heart of all things.
Hole, my country, my matter, my toasty-warm god.
Hole, stay eternal! All things endure a life of nuisance through small uteruses then die for the sake of the eternal life of a big uterus. Dear queen ant's many uteruses packed inside that high mountain: my eating and breathing has to do with my worship of the hole. This is my lifelong commemorative hole rite. Please get up, Your Highness, it's morning. Here is a fresh cup of coffee. Please calm down, Your Highness, it's nighttime. Here is a glass of wine for your fluttering brain. When he made me by blowing his breath into a hole, he who has created the world by drilling a hole into misery, the stink of his breath was overwhelming; today, I want to make him starve.

Wind, please stroke the alveoli of my lungs as you would a sick child. Please relay the message that time's pimp has not died; it still lives here. Please relay the message that the hole remains eternal from its previous life to its next life. Please relay the message that the hole gives birth to a hole and is raising a hole. (But who else is listening to what I'm saying besides my hole?)

O

All together: Dear Hole has died
               Dear Hole has resurrected
               Dear Hole lives again

(Holes eat and drink)

O

At midnight, the kids, still wet behind the ears, head to head with the hole's entrance inside the subway are screaming, swallowing, tremtremtrembling, and barking that the entire subway spurts up like fountain water, smelling fishy.

Inside the subway station, a child holds out his dirty hands.
He says he will be good. He says he won't be bad again.
I see the child at the station for several weeks.

At the hospital across the street, a hole is giving birth to a hole.
Please allow the safe delivery of a hole!
As a mother hole of a mother hole prays rubbing her two palms together, a soprano climbs up an organ made of hospital drainpipes in the delivery room, panting, then lets out a scream towards the sky. Dear Big Hole, please spit it out! This hole can't possibly handle a newborn. Please spit it out, Dear Big Hole! (Who decides the time of birth? Is it the baby? the Mummy? the Stars?)

A life sprouts from the fugue raging in the hallway of the hospital. It's nearly midnight.

Another manhole humanity is born. Time makes a hole in the baby's body.
Time puts a manhole's lid on the baby's head.

Down below at the restaurant, the chef's hands are in motion! With both hands he hacks away at the bodies piled up on the cutting board; there is nothing to distinguish one from another – plants and animals, jealousy, solitude, and spirit.

When I eat them tomorrow morning, does it mean that I will be eating my hole's skin? Eating my hole's outside? Eating my hole's tether? My hole's desire to persist, the music performed by commas has no pauses, hurhurrah!

O

The hole's essence is such that it's empty like the empty space inside of a flame. Tongue is that place, not wearing any underwear, it hangs onto the hole's end where there is nothing and licks and makes o o o sounds.

Therefore, to say regulate your desire means to regulate well the empty space, the inside of a blood sausage!
Goodness, how am I suppose to regulate a place that's invisible!
The factory supervisor who sits inside the hungry sausage – what does he look like?

O

At the intensive care unit, one floor below the gynaecology ward,
an electrical cord is plugged into a hole, a graph chart rotates waahwaah, the
heart beats bambam, then later the hole dies. Time of death: 12 minutes past
midnight. One handless watch stops.
The watch burns when the holes of the dead sag from greeting happiness for
the first time.
Skin remains and is placed in the drawer of a freezer and a hole filled with
happiness floats in air.

O

Dark tunnel before death
White tunnel after death

O

What nonsense, you say? Love comes out from where, you ask?
How can love come out from this hole then go into that hole, you ask?
Clear away the smelly hole, you ask?

O

Mummy manhole pats a baby manhole as if she's tapping on the stovepipe.
What a strange manhole!
It even has two holes from which tears gush out waah waah waah whenever
it's hungry.
Its two nostril-chimneys wail chugchugpuffpuff.
Every time the baby manhole cries, mummy manhole plays a bandoneon,
stretching then pressing, her tango musician hands in motion!

After the pipe connecting to the baby manhole was cut, it caused complications
in mummy hole's blood circulation and made her break out in blue rashes, so
she had to go down to the lower level of the hospital to repair her hole.

Baby is this hole
Mummy is that hole

Like the swimmers who each swim in separate lanes
the holes across are all different places.

O

Washbowls and bedpans on hospital beds make loud noises
and the inside of the mattresses fill up with reddish abdominal fluids.
Fluorescent lights with lots of dead flies inside their casings bleach empty
corridors blue and nurses throw into the sewer things the damaged holes have
vomited.
Manholes with hats on them that look like white clouds!
There is a rumour that those holes carry a drug-resistant strain of blood-
poisoning virus.

O

Try relaxing your legs and raising your hands above your head
to attain the posture of the rising steam.
Imagine that all the holes of your body are opening.
Think of your solid body changing to a liquid body and then to a gas body.
Unwind the additions, multiplications of your holes.
Try and picture your body whirling down the drain.
Then imagine the blue sky sitting on the holes, relieving itself!

My legs and arms dangle all over from the big drainpipe
and a heavy manhole lid is on top of my neck!

A girl is crying in her sleep, for she took a wrong step and fell into a hole.
The girl crawls into the deepest part of a cave.
A headlamp lights up a ravine between my body and soul
like a mole digging into dark earth.
I'm looking for the girl. Like a snail she crawls under a huge rock.
IV solution drops plopplop, trying to make a hole in my cave.
A lit mirror passes by glancing at my one-floor body.
Here, at times as one, insects, reptiles, rodents, mists, galaxies with wasted
nerves surge upwards as monsters, but today for some reason only the girl's
cry can be heard.

Look here, says the doctor
The hole's joint is constricted

What kind of melody from the hole is the ECG's machine connected to?
What kind of melody from the hole is the lie detector connected to?

O

Black smoke rises from the hole. It's the smoke from my own burning.
I shoot up! Up! A black maze, the unending spiral that begins at my feet.
The black smoke that has travelled through the hidden rooms inside the maze
wails, thundering beneath the clogged sky.

My face, my hair swirl and get sucked into my hole.
I get sucked down the storm drain.
At that moment, I try to remember who it was that sat in each dirty room
that was plunging down!
Do I hear the quivering sound of calling that room from this room? Do I hear
myself calling me from the outside?
Who is that person getting soaked in black rain, hanging onto a thin rope
above a bottomless abyss?

Why does my sleep that is solely mine return at last from elsewhere?
Why does my love that is solely mine return at last from elsewhere?
Why does my misery that is solely mine return at last from elsewhere?

Misery, where did you come from?
What what did you burn and run back like this?
Are you me? Who's this?
Why is a train living inside a hole?
Am I being derailed by the train along with the rhythm of it saying Love You
Love You?
The train that has taken all those many passengers to death!
A tunnel goes around inside the dark mountain and the train passes by me
like a storm.

Should I starve the train to death?

O

Love that is about a hole, a hole for the benefit of a hole, according to a hole.
I use the hole as I pretend to talk about love. I use the hole as I pretend to
talk about sadness. I use the hole as I pretend to talk about you. I use the
hole as I pretend to talk about myself. I use the writing of the hole, the hole
according to the hole, for the benefit of the hole. I stop and look into my
body. It's a mask that surrounds the hole. The rise and fall of civilisation
leaves a pattern on the mask then disappears. When the mask is ripped up,
there is no hole. I try walking. All kinds of grotesque structures around the
architecture of the hole walk rattlerattle. I walk holding up my neck stiffstiff,

not even stepping with two hands on the ground like a cow or a bitch. I'm a mixture, an upright sound, that gets poured into the mould that is 'nothing.' I'm a weak structure into which anxiety can easily intrude. Finally, I bow daily to victorious 'nothing'! My flesh! In India people greet each other as the 'god inside you' by saying Namaste. Who is pulling the trigger attached to my body just replicated from the mould?

This hole is structured in such a way that its exit sucks in its entrance. Death is designed to suck in birth. It was widely known that one of the princes of the Chosôn Period was born without an exit. Because it was against the law to make a hole in the prince's body, he died. Inside the hole's structure, my time gets excreted nonstop. I am swallowed by the hole then get excreted as a hole.

O

One side of the first apple bursts and gets sucked through the lips of the naked first woman. The original woman's yellow teeth and smelly tongue begin to grind the apple into small bits. Cold wind, suns, apple blossoms, the gentle strokes of rain on my cheeks all get sucked into a wormhole. The apple doesn't know where it's going, but it follows the general theory of relativity and gets swept down a funnel. A legend spreads, that time-travel becomes possible if you go through the funnel. A legend spreads, that if you leave here and arrive in the distant past and kill the lethal snake, I will get to stay in the vast spaciousness, the time of being unborn. In order to digest this hole, an adequate amount of yin mass is needed. Digestive juices are quickly produced inside the hole.

Empty my hole. Amylase enzyme. Vesta digested aid. The hole secretes digestive juices and mixes them with whatever it sends down. After it ingests the apple, the pitiful hole gulps for more towards the emptiness. It flails about like a snake that has fallen into the sea.

O

Hole is the prostitute of sky world
Hole is the second wife of emptiness
Hole is the prostitution cave of time
Hole is the scout of sleep
Hole is the soldier of farewell

The hole's architecture has no floors. So it's the deepest in the world. There is no one who can fill the hole's architecture.

I get sucked into the deep hole of oblivion, like when a little pianist in front of a piano suddenly gazes into the universe of music and glances around the galaxy's scarf, like when the rain that falls on a coastal city doesn't get to live even for a few minutes on earth but swirls down the drain and reaches the sea in an instant. I become distant and distant again. 'I cry out to you, Lord, from a deep place!' (Shout twice)

O

At one point a rumour spread that, if you can digest all the rats living in the hole, you could reach nirvana and wouldn't ever have to be born again. An afternoon of a woman already pregnant with the next life walking waddlewaddling by. Packs of rats are bartering me in my hole. I hear a chorus of rapid breathing.

Do you know that as you walk into the backlight, you are a hole floating in air? I who walk you am another hole? The inside of your hole is infinite?

O

Sometimes, a woman living in a hole can pop out from it.
A deep-sea woman hasn't been exposed to light before. She's a red skinless monster.
She has a round face, exhausted by the whirling of time.
Her heart is hanging from a street lamp, so sometimes an entire alley can echo boomboom.
Sometimes my blood becomes cold and my shadow and I swap bodies.
There are no holes in a shadow. Shadow is an afterlife.

O

I get on an elevator and press the button for basement parking. As I leave the hospital, my hole writes. It writes with a fine point, dark henna ink flowing out from it. A dream scooped up by the hole's abyss writes. A woman in the hole stretches her arms and legs outside the hole and writes. She makes the hole cry and shrieking words pour out from her. Her tongue jumbles them up. But my words go outside of me then return to my hole. The flowers in my hole fade as I shout, Flowers are blooming, flowers are blooming.

O

The verbs I use for cooking my hole are: 'boil, roast, steam, simmer, decoct, burn'. The objects used before the verbs are like the 'inside' – the innermost heart, cabbage stuffing, blood sausage filling. You cook my 'inside'. You cook it well – my empty place which is like the inner part of an onion. I don't know how to stop my 'inside' from burning up, so I always end up burning my invisible wick. Even when I boil my 'inside,' strangely, my heart becomes sick. You cook with '+heat' and '+water' based verbs, and the more you add '+heat' '+time' to the verbs, the more smoke rises from my hole and my heart gets cooked in the order of 'boil, roast, steam, simmer, decoct, burn'. In the end my whole body gets burnt. When you make my heart burn, my body also burns. The wall between my heart and body melts. The melted wall mushrooms again. Solid becomes gas. For your information, flower is a gas. It's a single-stemmed red gas. Heart is simultaneously a recipe and a cooked dish. When the smoke that burnt my heart pushes its way into your hole, you throw your chopsticks at it and say Go Away, You Stink! But then you don't particularly care for a sliced-up raw heart like a raw fish.

Today's dish – put several roots of hatred, add my mashed hole, and mix in shadow powder. Then boil the mixture down.

O

The holes of my body tremtremble when I follow the back of the truck fully loaded with holes.
Holes! Whose body will you become?
The round darkness inside the holes!
Transparent tongues pant, for they want to become holes!

O

The hole is screaming. It's screaming on the phone. It's picking its nose. The hole is deep in thought. It's sneering at something. It's ramming into something. Behind the car many other cars line up. The hole doesn't get shoved.
It holds back its tears, unable to vomit. Vomit and gastric fluids have reached the hole's neck. A police officer wearing leather gloves comes running.

O

'I' is a name for a place of confinement in my body!
'I' is a name for all the things that don't appear outside the body's hole!
'I' is a name for the lady and gentleman who don't recognise the person who lives in the body!
But is my hole sick? Is the mask of the hole sick?
If the hole dies, 'I' die too. So 'I' is a name for a single ripple etched onto a lake. It's a name for a woman confined inside the hole's architecture.

Therefore, once again I'm a hole. I 'do' hole. I'm someone who 'does' a hole voluntarily. All things are holes. All things 'do' holes. All things have just died, but the holes are alive. Holes will exist in the past and did exist in the future. I'm the hole's playground, I'm the hole's misery, I'm the hole's porter.

O

Red sap, bloody pus, mites are stuckstuck on the inner wall of a hole that leads up to the flower. The yellowish sebum, bloody pus on a newborn's skin. The small hole begins to rot. The hole gets bigger and bigger. Eventually the flower's head droops. The flower faded away after it tried to etch ripples in the air. Not a single cluster of the steam's ripples are visible – I wonder where they went after they floated in the air for a brief moment.

O

Dear Water! Fire! Wind! You who go up and down
the pitch-black starless alley, the chimney, the dark hole,
if you want to warm up the hole's darkness, you must get out of the body!
'There are so many repulsive people here. Let's go to a place where there is no one.'
Why do people always say the same things?

Beneath my hole, the graves are wide open like laughing mouths.
Here, noxious gas and filthy water flow.
I go into my body and suffocate.
If I go through the entire hole, I will fall into a grave.
The hole is a stovepipe made with the vastness of the universe.
At the innermost part of the stovepipe, there is a stove, my heart.

O

Clean up the hole! God commands that not a single rat should be left in the hole.
A train loaded with rats arrives at my hole. Packs of rats run rampant.
I quickly put the hole in a coffin and nail it shut.

O

You who writes a letter of longing
is your name Gall Bladder? or Small Intestine?
If not, is it Esophagus?
Your name is a nameplate glued onto a hole.
I even have to love your hole.

You are a theatre of hollowness.
Hole's church.
Hole factory.
I look at your face and can foresee the architecture of your hole.

Your tongue trembles delicately like rose moss
then the petals dangling at the end of the hole call my name as they fall.
So let's forget about the sewer today.
Your hole and my hole elegantly whinewhine.
Whining is the communication to and fro within the hole.

O

Hole, my beggar.
Hole, my prince.
Hole, my steel-enforced concrete that allows my body's movement.
Hole, my distant mandala.
The smooth traffic of the hole – that is existence.
Hole is my path, my truth, my beginning and end, so try your best to 'do' a
hole for your hole.
My hole's identity, my hole's solitude, my hole's addiction.
Who's sitting in the control tower of my hole?
I go into my hole's maze, leaving a trail of thread. It's a longlong winding path.

Yet, today, I want to send you down my path and have you implanted.
I want to live with you in my sewer.
A killer whale goes around the earth once then leaves again with its young.
At a deep place inside the hole, I slosh about like a well from which warm
water spouts up. I throb.

Hole labour – this is life.
Hole is the time bomb you have thrown.

You put your hand into my hole and stir.
Rose moss rollrolled up like a tongue at the end of the hole bloom.
The petals drool and dart their tongues towards my inside and outside.
The flower mixes the words, stirs the fragrances, and feeds the seeds to keep
them alive.
Again, for your information, the flower is a door. The door is a gas. It's
neither inside nor outside.
But then why do I have to spit out the seed to the outside only?
It's pointless pouring water into a jar whose bottom has fallen out. But the
flower only blooms in a jar without a bottom.

O

Keep the holes at a distance.
Abstain from the holes.
All holes are wolves.
The lessons of hole rabbis.

The night when my hole howls at the moon, I hold onto it and fall asleep
listening to its song.
When my hole sings the song in my knees, in my lymph nodes, in my pelvis,
in my groin, in my throat, in my nostrils, in my ears, the hole of the continent
over there replies.

A Tibetan pulls out one of my femurs and polishes a flute with it.

In a dream my song gets on a plane and flies through your hole, then lands.

I whimperwhimper and take off the hole as if taking off a heavy coat.

Music begins as I take off the hole. The imprisoned music unwinds the silk
from its cocoon. The music traveling through the veins flows out at the end
of the pen. Dear Hole, open the door. My hole doesn't open without my
body's 'doing'. Dear Hole, 'do' a hole. My hole opens as it opens yours.
Music gushes out from the hole. The hole listens to the music. The music
excavates all the graves hidden in the maze of my hole. The pipeline passing
through the middle of the music begins to tremor.
I need to tear your flesh to be able to listen to the music. With no hope,
comfort, or meaning I soar up then fall deep down along with the tremors.
Deep down there, the gigantic hole that has discarded its skin becomes even
bigger. At that moment,

I drink butter by the Genghis Riverside and burn up like a corpse with a
wick stuck down its throat. The dark lonely holes that my life has passed
through begin to spew out candle drippings. Flame begins to flare up from
the peak of the hole, which I refer to as this moment. Now at this moment
fire gets kindled in the pit of the mound of my body, and the flames flare up
along with the endless rapid currents of extinction. A flower blooms at one
point in time. The mandala of flames wavers about at the plaza of darkness.
When I go over the hole's climax the song of a song, the shout of a shout
flow out by themselves. All the holes of my body, cry! Blood vessels burn till
they turn white, my throat burns till it turns white.

A song flies up outside the hole.
The lids of manholes float in the air for a brief moment like graduation caps.

O

Dance is the sadness called upon by the music of my hole.
Dance is the cry that is called upon by the music rising up through my hole.
I dance like a pair of starved pink shoes that show up after midnight in the street.
I have come out of the hole, but my body is wearing a hole, the hole endlessly
proliferates!
I must dance all the mazes.
I need to dance till the hole becomes sublime.
The hole dances like a snake with a feather attached to its head, rising up.
The tunnel, the tornado, the distant path have a song in them.
My hole dances. The flame dances. The ash that burnt me dances.
Hole, disappear into the dance!
The hole without hands or feet dances. It dances like incense. The sewer
beneath my feet screams out sighs, and the wind pleads. Oh my god! All the
leaves on the trees along the street are your ears.
When I lift up my lowly hole towards the sky, the golden spacecraft takes off
from the hole.

I cry, laugh, shout at the square. My lips burst like a fountain. Sadness bursts.

The hole is emitted nonstop to the outside. The mandala of rhythm floats up
for a brief moment.
The sky lifts up my manhole's lid and starts a fire in my hole that is filled
with indescribable rhythm.
Like a surfer I pass through the golden waves.

Then, soon, I plunge down like a hawk hit by an arrow, a snake that has lost
its feather.
The world kneaded by music gets absorbed into the ground like spilled water
on the street.
The luminous dots of the music that used to go up and down at the edge of
the hole die like meteors.
The birds in my sleeves die. The sand mandala crumbles under the broom.
The coldcold charcoal, the night of the black shield rushes in.

O

There is a tunnel made by waves in Hawaii.
The tunnel was made by gigantic waves
that surge up then crash instantly in a circle.
When the blue sea lets out a sigh, the sea turns inside out
and the surfer on the yellow board goes through the sigh
The blue tunnel opens, yet crumbles!
One rolled up hole roams in the deep wave.

Horizon

Who split
the horizon?
The mark of the division between sky and land
A night when blood water seeps out from the space between

Who split
the space between the upper and lower eyelid?
The mark on my body from the division between outer and inner vastness
At night tears spurt out from the space between

Can only wounds permeate one another?
The dusk descends as I open my eyes
A wound and another wound merge
so crimson water flows endlessly
and the exit called 'you' shuts in darkness

Who split
the white day and the black night?
She becomes a hawk by day
and he becomes a wolf by night
We pass each other like knife blades
the night we meet

Sand Woman

The woman was pulled out from the sand
She was perfectly clean – not a single strand of her hair had decomposed

They say the woman didn't eat or sleep after he left
The woman kept her eyes closed
didn't breathe
yet wasn't dead

People came and took the woman away
They say people took off her clothes, dipped her in salt water, spread her thighs
cut her hair and opened her heart

He died in war and
even the country parted somewhere farfar away
The woman swallowed her life
didn't let out her breath to the world
Her eyes stayed closed even when a knife blade busily went in and out of her

People sewed up the woman and laid her in a glass coffin
The one she waited for didn't arrive, instead fingers swarmed in from all
    directions

The woman hiding in the sand was pulled out
and every day I stared vacantly at her hands spread out on paper
I wanted to get on a camel and flee from this place

In every dream the woman followed me
and opened her eyes
the desert inside her eyelids was deeper and wider than the night sky

Starfish

I leave my starfish in the Pacific Ocean
my cuckoo in Tibet
my sloth in the forests of the Amazon
and I cook and lecture and age like this

I tie my fingers to a pine tree in the tundra
and bury my eyes beneath the snow of the North Pole
and leave my heart to melt in the abyss of the Pacific Ocean
and I cook, eat, sleep, drink, and even laugh like this

Therefore sadness blows in from Sumeru
Cold tears arrive from the bottom of an ice sheet that stays frozen
all year long
Therefore fever arrives from the Sahara
from a faraway place overgrown with cacti that can't close
their mouths, for needles stick out from their tongues
the inside of my open mouth is hot as lava

So don't keep coming to me, my starfish, crazy starfish
It is said that you were made from a fleck of rice
and can become as big as a house, a mountain top
Don't return here even if a ditch forms from the tears
that I shed every night missing you
the ditch is no place for you to live
If you keep coming back I'll pin a star to my hair
and all the nights of the world will explode inside me

A fine new day arrives like a clear sky after the typhoon
When I stand in the street, wearing a pair of dead gutter-rat shoes,
my butterflies blow in from all over even though my body is so small
Why are my arms, my head, my legs so distant?

I must have been chased by all the wind in the world and gotten wrecked
inside this body
My arms and legs dissolve in all directions
my head feels hazy

Since I always lack oxygen, my footsteps move across the tundra
Being on time is my sickness, but I need to get going to be on time

Someone stares into me for a while then flees
My feet are outside of my vision

My feet gradually fade away and
take off like wolves into the distant mountains

NOTE: Starfish [*Pulgasal*] is the name of a monster from a fable, a monster that can only be killed by fire. According to the fable, during the Chosŏn period (1392-1910 CE) when Buddhism was suppressed by King Yi Sŏng-gye, monks were imprisoned. One monk created an animal from a fleck of rice, and the animal escaped from the prison and roamed the entire country eating iron bits and turned into a monster. In Korean *Pulgasal* and starfish are homonyms.

Seoul, Kora

The mountain barks
then follows me

The mountain gives birth
The mountain licks a mountain
The mountain's litter sucks on its nipples
The mountain cold-heartedly discards all of its litter
The young mountains copulate in broad daylight, the stench
The mountain roams like the pack of dogs inside a maze

The mountain looks at me with its wet eyes
It trembles as I stroke its neck
The mountain gets dragged away with a rope around its neck
The mountain gets locked up behind bars. It's beaten. It's kicked.
It dies.

The mountain eats shit, eats a corpse
The mountain, the rash-covered mountain attacks me with its flaming eyes
The mountain, the snow-topped mountain cries
The mountain without a single tree laments with its head flung back towards the sky
The mountain bites and fights a mountain
The mountain, the big mountain chases its own tail

Empire's military exterminates the mountain that swarms
The mountain that survived, the mountain, the mountain climbs over a mountain
and runs away
It's still running away

The mountain, the mountain that wants to shed a mountain, brings its hands
together and stretches them towards the faraway mountain, touches its forehead,
pulls them down to its chest, looks at the faraway mountain once again as it draws
its elbows to its waist, then bends its right knee, both hands down on the ground,
then bends the left knee, presses down its hands on the ground and then stretches
them out, then prostrates, its entire body touching the ground. Then it cries.
The mountain circles a mountain, repeats the whole thing every three steps.

NOTE: Kora refers to a loop of prostrations around the sacred mountain, Mt Kailash, in Tibet.

Onion

Under the tap a man peeled a woman's skin
The woman cacklecackled and peeled easily like an onion
As a layer of dark night peeled off transparent day soared
Blood draindrained down a pipe
like the mushy inside of a fresh egg
Someone cried, stopitstopit why are you all acting this way?
When day gets suckled the sadtastingspicytasting night soars
Day and night kept this up for a thousand ten thousand years, for all eternity
yet the woman peeled layerafterlayer
The man who peeled an onion cried because of its sap
and the woman cried along with him
ah andsoregardless today's day left and night arrived
yet I didn't know where I was
maybe I was hidden somewhere between the spicy layers
so when I kept asking where I was and turned around
the woman's body was just as before
and the man kept crying and crying and peeled the woman's skin
After I was all peeled like an onion, I wasn't there anymore
but the I that used to call me I was hiding somewhere
Night hid and trembled under the wood floor after taking off its spicy skin
yet the sea endlessly took off and put on a pair of pants
and yet it was hotinsummer and coldinwinter and everything drifted away
Isn'tthisthemostbeautifulstoryintheworld?

First

The thing that I envy most in the world is your first.
The thing that you envy most in the world – I wouldn't know.
Your first that seeps out from your sleeping face.
The thing that you brought here when you came from there.
I want to cut off your first.
What thing inside your face do I envy?
What thing? I wouldn't know.
Perhaps a thing like the very first milk from your mother who made you.
Your first that is made from such an ingredient.

You open a photo album and look at your first. The first inside the photo is
probably thinking of you. Thinking that it is thinking of you. Your beloved first
is hiding inside the photo but your hand floats the train on top of the open field
of the computer keyboard and touches first, first, first, first, each train car. Your
first. Where is it hiding?
Your first that is shy and hot as steam from mummy's milk that spouted into
you long ago. Your first that shuddered lumplump and became your body. The
tickle you felt when you met your first like when a flock of geese flies into the
sunset. Because you are now writing a farewell letter to me, your first is laughing
quietly? Perhaps it is thinking harder about you inside the photo? Your first
terrifying solitude that used to crouch and hang onto the inside of mummy's
tummy. First love that used to share and eat such solitude. There is a knife
inside the hearts of all the firsts of the world. There is nothing that is more
heartless than first. First always dismembers. First forever dies. Dies in an instant
as it is called first. A wedge of your lip that first has severed then runs away.
First, first, first, first. Your two wrists without a body run alone above the train
tracks of the keyboard, you and your first. A dog with two necks barks and roams,
searching under the hazy moon. The forgotten didn't know it was forgotten.
Died. Your first is dead. First that still flaps about inside your forehead.

Your first, my first, firsts that part forever.
I approached you as if
I were meeting you tonight for the first time
and had lost my first.
Did you also?
Then shall we hold hands and kisskiss?
Should I say it like that?

And at that time your first is the finale, flower, fracture.
Died. D e i d. Dide.
Shall I say it like that?

Beneath Mount Sumeru

A rock swells out of a rock
on the faraway mountain
the rock barks woof woof then retreats
Soon after the rock closes up

A dog, its whole body, swells out of Buddha's face
at the temple beneath the mountain
and barks woof woof then retreats
The instant a tranquil smile lands on Buddha's face
I can see a mouse being chewed up inside Buddha's lips

In the blue sky that peeled off layer after layer
the dog that had been smoked all day
barked woof woof sadly as though it were spewing out fire
then it ran off after turning the snowy mountain red
and at the temple beneath, the water in an iron pot
bigger than a lake boils gentgently
The sky's whitestwhite pack of dogs
falls into the iron pot

The wild dogs that come out of me cry all night long outside the tent
I beg plead and bark
Please let me in I want to go inside
When I open the tent to look up at the moon, the dogs' saliva
drips down white upon all the valleys of the mountain peaks

I can hear the voice of someone I dislike in my throat
At the temple beneath the mountain, Buddha's torso shrinks
every time I bark wo oof woof
Now the golden Buddha has become as small as a toad

Silk Road

I paid a visit to my fever during my break

Here I carried a baby on my back and kisskissed it
As the flesh scent that smelled like gourd flower slowly ripened
a message intermittently arrived saying that my suffering was boiling in that place
all alone, covered by the stench of urine and feces under the scorching sun
I who have concealed that place am going inside it
like a camel that pantspants showing all of its gums
Suddenly the fever came for me and pounded my insides and left
leaving a few words on a thin piece of silk that could melt
but later...... later...... as I ripened to mush
Out of the blue, after many decades, I went to visit my fever

In the desert the crazy sun
like the terribleterrible hydrogen bomb that is still going off
after it exploded in the year of my birth
pours out the shards that still glow from red to dark
I have never once received the touch of the rainwater
The old camel was carrying me up the black hill
where the rocks that had broken into pointed bits of quartz were piled up
I who have broken out in red spots
between the layers of fine silk
The white twigs that the camel had no choice but to chew
had thorns as thick as my fingers
and blood gushed out nonstop from the camel's mouth
I couldn't believe there could be such a place filled only with suffering
My daughter said that inside the mirage she saw
a Buddha that had attained nirvana
stretched out on its side inside a temple
but I had to swallow the tall deep-blue waves
that kept coming up through my throat
Every time I swallowed the waves, the red sand twister whirled inside me

There was a child who couldn't eat and sleep crying on the bed in the
emergency room
The child was so bandaged there wasn't any opening for the needle, the
tranquilliser and the mother called out the child's name nonstop, 24 hours a day
Yuni, Yuni, trying to pull the child's name from its body

After I got back from the desert I was lying on the bed in the emergency
room overcome with fever and I stared at my camel that was still climbing the
rocky black hill
I'm here, yet I watch the dirty camel climb the Flaming Mountains by itself
I tell the camel as I shudder, You go there and I'll go here, then at some point
we'll meet again at a pond near the sky
Inside my sleep, feverish, I gulpgulp down the blue mirage on my own

I Don't Rot Because I'm Crazy

The tepid bath water in the tub speaks
You are completely soaked in me
I feel every part of your body
like the music that goes inside your ears
but where are you?

The cooled water in the tub speaks
I've lost my hair
I'm bald
I don't have any smell either
but now I rot like this
through your smell

Music speaks
I don't have arms or hands
I can embrace even your sweat pores
but I can't catch you

I rot because of you
like the bath water
I curl around you and come out and die
like the soaked music

I die because you have forgotten me

The putrid water that comes up to your neck rots

Yes, finally it's the victory of the gutter!
It's the sky of guts! Hurhurray!
The tunnel beneath my feet!

All the Garbage of the World, Unite!

On the seat you left, two beer bottles, a cigarette butt, two pieces of scratch paper.
Why are you screening my calls, my messages? Don't you have anything else to do?
You are the bourgeoisie of communication. Why am I always so afraid of the
phone?
When you look at me, I always feel as if I should change into something else.
How about changing myself into a pile of clothes dumped on the sofa
or a pale pink wad of bubble gum dangling from someone's lips
like the poor tummies of all the animals that flail about when they are turned over?
Do you know?
Eyesnavelgod. Forearmsearflapgod.
Sweetpotatokneesappleseedgod. Pigstoenailschickgod.
Dreamingdivingbeetlesashtreegod. Lovelygirlsheelstoenailgod.
Antsghostscatseyeballgod. Ratholescatsrottingwatergod.
Mrsdustingarmselephantgod. Salivadropexplodeslikefreongas.
Salivafountainevenmoremortifyingnauseatingthanthesmelloflionsrottenbreathgod.
Do you know all the dearest gods that are hanging onto our limbs?
On the seat you left, a wet towel, a wad of gum, a crushed tomato.
Dear blackgarbagebags who thankfully lent each one of their bodies.
Dear foldedarms of the window and concrete and steel under my feet.
How high the armsofthemachinehammers that beat down steadily upon
those foldedarms.
All the pigs of the world unite god. All the cats of the world let's become a
butter god.
Dear wrists escape from the arms god. Heap of curses, mackerel corpses spit out
from a soccer player's mouth god. There are 3 million gods in India. How many
people live there?
Dearest multiple gods that have swarmed in from the sky, land, sea.
On the seat you left, I sit like a garbage god, and do you or don't you know
that I wait for the green truck heading to the landfill like the dearest dirtiest
loftiest god
that has survived till now because of its hunger for humans?
Do you or don't you know that every day our hair falls and mixes with the
melting water of an iceberg in the faraway sea?
Yournostrilssingledropofapricklynosehairearthgod!

Strawberries

A full plate of red tongues arrived

They quivered like the tongues of the choir members as they sang the hymns

Your tongue is placed on top of my tongue

Our tongues are getting goose bumps

We examined all sorts of tastes in the world, we returned at last
and gently bumped against the millet-like protrusions

You were like someone who had in your mouth only a tongue and no teeth

The achy root has spread between the intestines like lightning
and the coldestcold stream water flowed down your hair like electricity

I was afraid that the red water would rise if I bit down on the red things in
my mouth that my face had vomited endlessly, so I just kept them in my
mouth

The four arms as soft as the branches with snow on them became entangled
and gathered up a full plate of kisses!

I heard that all those tiny protrusions were my seeds only after I had mashed
your tongue

Knife and Knife

Knife loves a knife

it loves in the air like something without feet

The knife that has fallen in love is not a knife but a magnet

The knives' persistent gazes tug at each other and spin!

The drops of sweat disperse, the moans are spit out

It looks as if the two knives are going to lie down for a bit with their bodies crossed in the air, but their glittering eyes stare out in the same direction, somewhere distant

The moment they beat down on each other's body and aim for a hidden place, inside their gaze the beheaded cherry blossoms fall off every April!

The knife's love will only end when someone's body ends up on the floor

It can love without any rest like the dancer in red shoes, but it can't end its love

It can endure embracing the blue body, but in the end it can't part from it and go back

It can't come down or even fall down in the air

Blood spews out from the four stiffstiff knees

That body like mine is a hole, cut out that black hole, stab it till the inside overflows to the outside

Wash your face with the warm blood spewing out from the hole

This dreadful love never retreats no matter how much you scream

That is why my love keeps the blade's body up in the air

How shall I say it, that our love's feet never once touched the ground?
Is this a blessing, the fact that our love still hovers in the air?

Hum
Hum

The confessional's window looks like a beehive
The holes in the priest's mic also look like a beehive, they are all hexagonal
Every time the priest says blahblahblahblah
a swarm of bees falls out of his mouth
The smell of incense grows overpowering as the alter boy lights the incense
on cue
and the middle-aged choir ladies sing Ave Maria in unison with the priest
The ladies' mouths are all hexagonal-shaped
The saliva inside their mouths is sticky like honey

My mummy's voice is heard intermittently
between the swarms of bees pouring out of the receiver
Drivecarefully anddontdrinkandpartyaround andblahblahthisblahblahthat
When I turn around in the middle of the call and shout
Mute the TV
I see swarms of bees pouring out in the news my husband is watching
The fluttering wings of the bees on asphalt
where rain is beating down
I wonder how many bees live inside the motorcycle
that is carrying a bowl of noodles
I can't stand those bees
Bees swarm from the news announcer's throat
The bees' stingers cloud up the TV screen
As the swarms of bees fall out from the police officer's walkietalkie
the swarms that have lost consciousness pour out onto the closed eyes of the
motorcycle guy who is lying on the ground in the rain
In the rainy night the bees transmit the words in the air in a frenzy
Did the butterfly net burst, did the monitor burst, did my skull burst also?
I can't stand it everythingislikeswarmsofbees likeswarmsofbees

Swarms of bees swarm inside the words that begin with D
Dearpriest Dearteacher Dearjudge Dearmadam Dearuterus Drum D D D
washing machine

The washing machine is spinning hum hum
The fetus is suckled clean inside mummy's tummy
When I put my ears against her tummy, I hear the cries hum hum
the infant's kicking spinning
The priest instructs

Please recite Ave Maria five times before you leave
The confessional's window looks like a beehive
The two earflaps of the priest who peers out from the hole are like hexagonal
gelatin
The priest's black eyes squirm like two bees that have fallen into honey
their two sets of six thin legs wiggling about
Please leave quickly!
hum
hum

Trainspotting

As I stood at Tongni Station
I felt as if I had become that retired actress
who ran out onto the railroad tracks because her red dancing shoes wouldn't
come off
at a whistle stop where no one gets on or off

When it was time for the express train to pass
the whistle stop had goose bumps like the fishing boat that received a storm warning
and the mountains that sweated profusely spat out heaps of coal

The fact that even the whistle stop talks
The fact that the whistle stop wakes up from sleep, sweating from fever
The fact that the whistle stop even goes for a walk along the tracks deep in the
night
The fact that the whistle stop also falls down under the dark tree and weeps
The fact that the whistle stop sits in the corner of a tavern and pretends to be
waiting for someone
The fact that sometimes the whistle stop doesn't answer the phone

Will you let me off at Wedding Station?
or give my regards to Birthday Station every year
and if you don't want to do that, perhaps you could come to
my Funeral Station
Even here the cell phones ring nonstop

The sound of the hundreds of insects passing by all at once
sleepthengo crythengo drinkcoffeethengo haveadrinkthengo
furthermore throw away several train cars and go like an unmarried mother
discarding her baby
then when the whistle stop calls out Let me go with you! no one will turn around

The tickets from Seoul to Kangnûng have rusted yellow
inside the ticket box with many drawers
and I stare at the tracks quivering like a cello
that has grown infinitely tall
and when the freight train pulls on my loose string and lets go of it
the cold stars appear on my face and it starts to tingle
With my eyes I swallow every wooden block of the track that lies
like a corpse, that used to ride the endless shadows
as though I am unscrewing every screw of the metal band of my watch

The Water Inside Your Eyes

When I get up in the morning singing a sad song
the water in the cup feels sad, the toilet water feels sad
the vase water that gurgles up through the flower stem feels sad
and the water that patiently waits
filling the tap's mouth also feels sad

Don't say Fly up when you see the birds flying outside the window
because that is really me falling
and falling, endlessly falling
riding the earth that only knows how to fall
into the vast, empty sky

The flowing water washes its body as it flows
but a song as sad as this stagnates inside me
and can't flow out so the stopper cries
and the pipes below also cry

I am a body that is born to flow away
flow away to be born as water inside your body
It's alright that there is no horizon, no land for me to stand on
as long as I just get to go
I don't rest deep inside your body or overflow or whisper
I am born only to remain vacant like the water inside your eyes

Where did this sad song flow in from?
Why does it keep welling up and flowing over my rotting body?
Why does it make the water in my cup, the water in my flower vase cry?
The water rises up so high along the banks of the Han River
that not a single road sign is visible
Down below, deep beneath the riverbed
the sound of cold water flowing inside the underground cave

The ceiling shakes, the columns become wet
and the pots rust. I must open my eyes wide, pump out my chest
and hold my breath and go out
Maybe I need to take some naphthalene, so I won't rot
I need to find the key and get out of here

A Breezy Prison Breezes

1-hour-and-30-minute-long prison of my morning commute
Just because there is a window and headlights in front of me
no one knows about this solitary room that runs 70 miles per hour

I go to Room 301 then 401, over here then over there
The 50-minute prison, 100-minute prison, 150-minute prison blow in hard

The cube is even more unbelievable because it's softsoft
The fierce rooms swoop over me
They taste bitter and rancid like unripened chestnuts

Will the prison open
if I peel off those wet eyes stuck to the car window?
Those eyes are lighter than leaves
Those eyes are so resilient
Since those eyes don't peel off
if I pluck a star, a boundless world behind it would open up
that star is a gap but it won't move out of the way because it's crying
so this night, this dark wind tricks me, I don't know that I'm in prison
this night, the prison with a dark curtain flowing down separates you and me

So in this prison you must use emblems
For the prison to forget the prison it must keep telling lies
I rattle off lies in my lecture room

Saying The flowers blossom is to say It smells outside the prison
Saying Let's hold hands is to say I can't escape no matter what
Saying Let's kiss is to ask Did you hide the key?
Saying Sleep with me is to say I'm stuck with a life sentence

Just because there is a window, a wind is blowing, and starlight is leaking
I don't know that I'm in prison
After work when I lie down in my sleeping prison
all the prisons outside of the outside of the prisons run to me
and tie up my body with the redred blood-paths

10-hour-long 10 year-long 100 year-long prison

Why Are All Mermaids Female?

I prostrate myself on the floor and kiss my shadow
I bite off the shadow's ear

My shadow's eyes light up

A camel-like person who has never bathed once
hides in my upper body
a black shark-like person who
pulls me into the deep sea and roams about
hides in my lower body

I am a woman who is half eaten by the ancient people
with stinging whips in their hands

Therefore, on my tired face
a camel's eye stays open, bulging out
gazing blankly at the body of my next life
and the voluptuous curve of the sand hill
and hundreds of prickly fish scales
like unborn babies' fingernails
are stuck on my ankles
They never fall off

Someone shakes my arm and wants me to go far away to the desert

Someone ties my legs and wants me to go far away to the ocean

My warm tongue freezes first before my fingers
I stutter, It's cold, it's cold
Menstrual cramps fiercely engulf my lower body
It hurts, it hurts
I twist my body
half of it trapped in the desert
and the rest in the ocean

I bite my shadow's ears
I swim in myself all day

Why are all mermaids female?
Do they self-reproduce?

Why Is Mummy Salty?

When I wake up from thirst in the middle of the night at Mummy's house
a salt lace curtain droops down the porch window
Patterns made from whitestwhite salt
trail faintly down the wall
When I open the cupboard, the mounds of salt
shine white next to the upside down bowls
and salt accumulates like the first snow of the year on a dress I have taken off
When I open the attic door for no particular reason
salt pours out one sack, two sacks
When I put a single grain of salt into my mouth
my eyes say, It's salty it's salty, first, instead of my tongue
and two cold streams of water dripdrip
All my life I've done the best that I could, biting my lips
But, oh, what's all this again?
Outside the window a whitestwhite mountain of salt shoots up highhigh as if
there is no end to the sky and suddenly the glass in my hand shatters into bits
and as Mummy starts to wake up
the salt patterns that spread in all directions
vanish without a trace
like the multi-coloured sand mandala that is drawn and erased by the Tibetan
monks
all the salt gets swept into the deepestdeep night sea
Why is Mummy's house so salty?

Delicatessen

1

Father raised children
to eat them, of course
Father said,
My children's plump cheeks
are the tastiest thing in the world

My little sister kept a ball of needles beneath her pillow
so she wouldn't fall asleep at night
As a result she became a porcupine
Spines spilled out from her body as soon as she opened her mouth
My little brother became a bat
He only came out late at night and fluttered about
Be quiet when Father is having his dinner!
Tropical fish in the fish tank floated up like puckered lips
Mummy made soup with the red fish every morning
I became a skunk
When I'm disturbed I have a musky cough all day long

Father walked
carrying us in a black bag
Tears streamed out of it
So many tears flowed that it caused a flood
People from the village made a boat from a rubber bucket
and paddled with a spoon
Don't let Father cross!
Father couldn't reach the house because the river of tears was too deep

2

When we grew up we raised Father
to use him as a broom, of course
We carried Father and swept the ground in the yard
Sometimes we swept snow as well
Father smoked crouched on a dirt floor
His hair became thinner every day

Put the broom back inside!
How repulsive! When I got closer, I saw myself
My hair had thinned, and I was smoking
as I looked over my shoulder

And I raised Father
inside a warm adobe stove
to eat him, of course

To Swallow a Tornado

Have you ever swallowed a tornado?
A tornado is supposed to be swallowed through your backbone
My body flips over
my hair becomes as stiff as frozen laundry
and I feel goose bumps down my backbone

When my body becomes tight as a bow I can see everything
Your wound has exploded red so every valley has become a valley of blood
The blood-red light is the sin of staying alive by feeding on the living
so the red lips are in full bloom above the dark earth

My beloved, the last skeleton beneath your hair is already dead
The rake-like smile of the wind spreads
on the backs of the pedestrians walking hurriedly
God has clawed and gathered up the empty blankets
of those who have departed this world
and lit a blue fire far up above
The world is like transparent silk underwear
you can see right through it

Am I wind's home
or a tornado's host?
When the wind's path that is as cold as a snake
rises up from the deep place
my arms and legs flutter like the bamboo leaves on the day a typhoon arrives
and when my tears splattersplatter everywhere
a sad song comes up like a whirlwind from the inside of my body
Someone please come and hold my bow-like body
that keeps getting bent back

Have you ever swallowed a tornado?
Have you ever sat by the night sea and cried, I don't want to! I don't want to!
Have you ever swarmed out to the sea and thrown the pebbles hard
while listening to the waves shout, Take it, take it, take it?
Do you hear all the different screams of the million water droplets?
The spirits that don't want to leave cry so easily
Have you ever closed your fists tightly and withstood their cries?

Have you ever shouted, Go! Go! Go back!

An Old Woman

meme is a lone tree that got planted in a bed
a tree so huge that she can't see her entire body all at once
She's a tree that can't even turn over or rub with her fingers
when the first butterfly she has waited for tickles with its thin toes
the spaces between the grooves of her lips

meme's waist is so wide that she can't bend
over or lie down by herself
Someone must come and change
her underwear and diapers
'But it's all right, please just insert the pencil between my lips'
meme is a big tree
meme – she can get jealous and miss someone, but she can't even make
a single call
When I scratch meme's side it feels as though I am scratching
the thick skin of an old tree!

meme is a lone tree that can't go and die on her own
but loves most the fantasy of closing her eyes tight and curling herself into
a ball and escaping by going under the bed, under the drain, out of the Earth,
swirling out of the sewer

mememe is a lone tree
No one can walk beside her with head held up in the air
because of the stench she gives out when she cries before the first leaves of the
season sprout and the dogs lift their legs and piss on her lower trunk and take off

memememe is a lone big tree
Her stench of sadness when she cries before the first flowers of the season bloom
is so unbearable that my family members carry a bowl of medicine
and hold their noses outside the door

NOTES: **Double p – How Creepy** *(opposite page)*
oppa = older brother of a girl/woman
A strange custom has recently developed in South Korea. Women address their older boyfriends
as *oppa*, and married women with children call their husbands papa or daddy as their children
would.

Double p – How Creepy

pp they're so creepy that I can't stand it. pappaoppa they are so creepy that I can't stand it. Squeeze hard and have some honey, a gift from pappa, when I opened the lid of the beehive the wigglewiggling larvae filled each hexagonal cell, ahahahah it was like seeing pappa*oppa* larvae inside each hole of pp. Two of my married former students showed up with their husbands and one called her husband *oppa* and the other called her husband pappa – how creepy. I had no choice but to say, I'm leaving first I can't bear to hear any more of this kinship name nonsense. I'm so afraid of pp that I don't want to say happy or cute. I just feel great! great! I don't clap, yet I bite the emptiness. Maybe I'm a princess who has to live with smiles dangling from my face to keep my kingdom peaceful. I even hate soappy laundry because I hate pp. In my dream the washer is spinning roundandround, the wooden laundry stick beats down on the laundry splashsplash, and Mummy's scream gets sucked into the washer as she pulls her adorable babies out of it and throws them onto the floor. Whenever I dream this dream, I feel as if I'm pregnant with a wet-laundry-like baby. A while later a former student of mine with her cute *oppa* came for a visit and said that she had gotten a divorce and been in a mental hospital. 'I got divorced because my ex-*oppa* kept hitting me, but after the divorce I developed schizophrenia, so this time I screamed 24 hours a day as I was getting beat up by the *oppa* of my delusions, and I couldn't sleep or eat from all the beatings.' I despise pp so much. Every time I call out to pappa*oppa* I become ppreathless as if I'm standing in front of the ruins of Angkor Wat where the walls have crumbled and piled up on the ground. pp is even more disgusting than a burn with sprinkled black sesame seeds. pp is darkdark like a mouth closed around the two pupils of my eyes. Pappaisppad*oppa*isppreathless, pp is even more suffocating than kisskiss.

There is an apartment building with lights on and a tree in front of my window
At night people get sucked upp the stepps like the laundry in the washing machine
Thousands of lips hang from the apartment tree
Tens of smelly teeth hide inside each lip
Apartment tree trembles like an aspen tree and sings
Thousands of ears hang from the apartment tree
The inside of the ears is filled with screams made of smelly vowels
that have turned to pus
Please don't ppull the plug of the apartment tree
What if the plug is ppulled and the sppinning laundry wet with tears
falls off in droves like the leaves of the aspen tree?

Tearfarming

Ice princess appeared in a dream for several days running. Before long I found myself staring vacantly at the ice princess even in my waking hours. The ice princess lived somewhere over there on the snow-covered mountaintop. She lived and commanded echomaids. The echomaids didn't allow anyone to come anywhere near where they lived. When hello! came, hello!maids sent back hello! When hurrah! came, hurrah!maids sent back hurrah! When a thump! arrived, thump!maids hid the thump inside a lump of ice. Have you ever seen an ice princess with tears hanging like gigantic melted candles from her cheeks? Have you ever heard that an ice princess is tearfarming over there? When the ice princess cries a lot it's June and when she stops it's October. When the ice princess stops crying no one steps out from the mud huts, and the animals crouch down in their nests and keep chanting, *ommanipadmehum ommanipadmehum*. No one can get around on the road or the gravel lot. Then when June arrives the echomaids open the shed door. Then tears become a huge river and flow down a rocky mountain. People herd sheep and migrate along the flowing tears. A land shaped like a green fan appears next to the valley of the rocky mountain. Down below in the lowest desert, an oasis overflows. Then the farmers step on the teardrop-like blue barley and black dirt with their bare feet. Finally the donkeys parched in winter get to take a bath. Patchpatch of yellow rape flowers bloom on the rocky mountain. Remote mountains yellyell, a thousand fierce tearfalls hanging from them. Large animals come out of the cages and travel farfar away. As they leave, the ice princess sobs even more. She cries so hard that her hair is in danger of falling out. Her eyes form without eyelids or eyebrows and then float away. The blackest eardrums inside the whitest ears float up so high that the sky becomes dark blue. And that is when the ice princess is kicked out. Someone who ventured up near where the princess lives, frozen except for the blood in his body, returned and said that he saw the ice princess, her entire crushed body limplimp, being kicked out after she had spilled all of her whitest tears. Dark blood gushed out as the ice princess walkedwalked to dye a mound of stones black. That someone who saw the ice princess had both of his eyes put out. As I heard the princess for the first time beneath the snow-covered mountain, my mind hazed over. Even if I live for a thousand years, her wretched scream will linger in my heart. After I met her restless and painful expression, even in my waking hours, I stared at the ice princess with the icy tears streaming out of her eyes. I'm becoming so thirsty that I could drink a thousand, ten thousand buckets of ice princess's tears.

The Himalayas Said To Me

Take a look at the deep-sea fish
Their feet are stuck to the bottom and stay stuck their entire lives
For them, being born means sinking deep down
all the way to the bottom, falling for a lifetime

Take a look at the deep-sea fish
Look at their bodies stuck to the bottom like an engraved print
They are dark, not a single drop of light leaks from them
Look at those dark lumps, lumped by loneliness
The water pressure must be horrendous
The woman comes up carrying a knapsack
her panting lips stay parted

Take a look, I've lost my ring in the abyss
A meteor falls and hits the ocean
My snow flurries can never reach the inside of the deep, deep water
My heart that has floated above the surface flutters
They say that something that has once flowed away never returns

Take a look, below the horizon far away
The woman carrying a knapsack comes up
Red sunset, waves of blood on the painting woman's
white pants splash about inside and outside of her
The feet of the deep-sea fish only get unstuck from the bottom when they die

Rainy Season

The ghosts always gripegripe
The women who met an undeserved death are the noisiest among them
A crazy ghost unexpectedly comes dripdrip quietly
A female ghost who has fallen for her first love comes somewhat fiercely
for the lightning attaches itself to her hair

Don't pound on the lake too hard
Blood water surges out of all the places where you pound

That woman who has worms coming out of her mouth
please don't hit her too hard
One sack, two sacks of worms fall out of her mouth
because she gets beaten every single day
Later she even pukepukes out her intestines
and her empty body gets mashed
Oh the stench

Have you ever had a bad encounter with a ghost that died in the forest?
The ghost pulls out from its mouth vines that stretch endlessly
and blue tongues dangdangle from the vines
and those tongues chatter all night long
the ghosts are so tirelessly noisy
they leave then return
they come looking for you even when you chase them away
They gripegripe and their sweat splatters over heaven and earth
like the smoke that fills the house on a memorial day

The lake has opened thousands of its mouths and begins to chatter
Who will plug up those red mouths now?
Oh all of heaven and earth is a lake, it's red

Cinderella

Our city is made of ice
An ice carriage slides on the ice pavement
Ice horses' manes stand up and glitter
Ice coachman skillfully wields the ice whip
Today is the day of the dancing ball
the ice bell rings from the ice palace
the ice chandelier descends like angels' toes

The trees are surrounded by the bluestblue sparkling ice
My beloved iceman dances trapped in ice then leaves
Our ice flesh mingled, loved, gave birth, and danced

The world we created is as blue as the infant's funeral march
People's gazes are blind and clean as if made from ice dew

Take a look around my world made of cold like the inside of a transformer
In the quiet ice room of the winter fish water boils in the ice teapot
No one can enter here but you and I

But the moment we are caught off guard
stepmothers' cold toenails dig into our flesh like icicles
The netherworld pretends to love us so much
It may be keeping us fresh only to pull the plug later
When we get slapped by a hand as hot as lead
our blood rots and our bodies fall like timber
In that world we can only pass through each other's bodies
like two converging cold winds

For us there is no future
only our vivid faces sealed in the ice
In our bosom the North Pole and South Pole happily embrace
and my ice slipper falls down the steps and freezes

But now it is time to return, the ice rooster lets out a long crow
I really don't want to go there where tears endlessly gush from my body
That place where the red flower has blossomed is where my heart was sewn
I never want to see that filthy place again

I killed the ice rooster all night long, Stop crowing! I gagged it
I plucked white feathers and threw them into the air
But now it is time to offer the whitest ice rooster to the ice palace and return

Heartless time drank the last glass of wine on the table
The last piece of ice glittered in your hand

The carriage speeds away and cries pour out like a snowstorm
Ice shoes melt, ice carriage melts
only the coachman holding a whip is left
The coachman asks, Damn it, why won't you stop crying?

Bright Rooms

The copy machine vomits out
sunflowers every second
No sooner do I turn around than
the room is filled with sunflower blossoms
All the flowers of the sunflower patch have copied
the sun so diligently that every one of their heads is bent
as if the ageless Sophia
were about to step out from the garden

My copy machine, every time I enter this square, bright box
it scattscatters the black bouquet of flowers that it has kept in its heart
into the air and smiles like the excavated mummy at Tutankhamun's pyramid
This is the room where the lips live, the lips I need to feed and make laugh
my bright room where the breeze and sighs go in and out incessantly!

Every time the copy machine lights up every second
and pushes and pulls my body
the inhaling breath goes in and the exhaling breath comes out

My face that has been copied onto thin paper
sits on the long seat of the subway train, line number 4
and falls into the faint light for the millionth time
My face doesn't even know where its original is
I have already become as faint as faint can be
I draw the route of my next commute

When I return home, I wash my face with a soap named Despise
and erase my face with a face cream called Deface
I who have been photocopied tonight
tear up my spiral notebook that got filed away
Do I ultimately live inside my body?
When I turn off the light switch in the bright room
where my final, barely photocopied smile stays afloat
the square copy machine box goes dark
and my body also grows dark as the inside of a coffin

Pinkbox

Pinkbox that has just arrived. Pinkbox that waits to be opened. When I embrace the box, it smells of a faraway place. But no one who goes inside can escape. Ah adorable pinkbox. Pinkbox, my first baby. Hello, pinkbox. I want to rock pinkbox in a cradle. (For your information, God doesn't know how to make anything rectangular.)

Folded pinkbox. I want to forget about everyone. Want to forget about Mummy and Daddy. I'll just lie down like a knife blade and dream only of revenge. Pinkbox has two hidden breasts that pull on the chest painfully. Blood streamed down pinkbox. This box is smaller than me. It's unbearably tight. Pinkbox has a bleeding pinkhole. Pinkbox will die if the tape is ripped and light is shone inside. I'm a sick pinkbox. I hated the pink all the time. It's useless to try and be heard outside the box. No one listens closely to what a box has to say. Rest, eat, forget, bell ringing box. Pinkbox can't speak, hear, or see under the deafdeaf blackboard. You need to become a sick pinkbox if you don't want to go to school. Look over there at the high-rise apartment building. In each box boxes lean and look out at the same boxes.

Dented pinkbox. Love has been a prisoner inside me since I was born. Someone gnawed at pinkbox like a cornered rat every time I couldn't see you. Pinkbox is still a pinkbox no matter how many times it gets folded. Pointless to ask pinkbox what's in the box. I'll become a pinkbox that sings, drifts about, and overflows when you arrive. I'll become a boat with a pink light, foaming its way through the rainy night. I'll become a boat of pink light carrying trees with leaves out to the widewide sea. Yet, life is nothing but a glance from a torn hole, a distant thing. I'm just an empty box, a discarded, crushed pinkbox.

Unfolded pinkbox. Has spit out all the precious writing like an old silkworm. When did this all happen? Like a lone plank of wood floating in the sea of pitch-black darkness. There's nothing. Pinkbox takes a lashing from the rain. Dirty toes dig in as pinkbox gets flattened in the underground passage. Pinkbox with cold hands and feet. When will I sink down?

Fallen pinkbox. Torn pinkbox, pinkbox cast away, it might be better to grab onto the horizon. Can't embrace it since it has parted far. *Dirty pinkbox, smelly pinkbox, crumpled pinkbox, flowing pinkbox.* Pinkbox covered with faded writing, dirty pink, old pink, open hole pink, flapping, its hair down pink. Like a camera, pink captures you, but there is nothing after the film is taken out. Don't let the box return. It's just dirty paper. Burn this box.

My Throat Has Become a Candlestick

When I lie and wait at the riverside it's my turn again, the river cleans my body, the heedless wind blows in and makes my white sleeves flutter, my tears dry up, you have washed your hair and have a white towel wrapped around your neck, you lift me up to the bed of flames, you pour butter down my throat and place a wick in it, you light the wick, my throat has become a candlestick, my organs burn up like beeswax, green flames shoot out from my mouth, outside the bed my feet shout, It's cold it's cold, you cover my chest with a layer of straw, you set fire to the straw, you sprinkle petals on me as though you occasionally think of me, you even throw incense sticks at me, as you ignite the floor's radiant heat I spit fire from my whole body, my ribs are burning, my muscles dance like when a scarecrow is thrown onto the bonfire, in the middle of the blaze I cry and scream and also suddenly stand up, I give birth to my death, I curl up, I'm in labour delivering death, when I'm done I even watch my burning naked body, the blaze escorts death to the wind, you scatter the ash by the river, you also take a handful of ash and taste it, I who have turned into ash don't taste good, I have no thought, now the ash no longer belongs anywhere in the world – sky, earth, and air, the ash make up a sack, two sacks, goodness, ten sacks, you keep staring at the river even when a mangy dog takes off with my eyeball that has become as big as the sky, you wash off the remainder of the ash with the water in the washbowl. Then you go down to the river to wash the ash from your body,

why do you poke at my thigh with a skewer?
why do you beat down on my head?
so you'll burn well

FROM

SORROWTOOTHPASTE
MIRRORCREAM

I'm OK, I'm Pig!

Pig Speaks

Anyway, to nail Pig on a cross would be too natural, meaningless.

I enter the Zen room, sit cross-legged and stare at the wall in order to meditate.

You know, I'm confessing right now, I'm actually Pig. You know, I've been Pig since birth. Filthy, I'm filthy, really filthy. A mind? I have no such thing.

I'm smart nevertheless. My IQ is the highest amongst mammals. I love cleanliness. I hate dreams of overflowing toilets. My IQ drops 30 points after having such a dream.

I snort like someone who has woken up from a morning nap submerged in filthy water.
I want to blow my nose but there's no tissue in the Zen room. Don't the monks ever have a runny nose?

You know, you, Pig, are also melancholic? The fact that Pig also has an expression? Your body fattened by mushy sorrow, filthy water, slippery-slippery muck.

At Kunsthal in Rotterdam, I saw Jan Benning's photographs of Sumatran grandmothers during the Japanese colonial rule, but there were only two kinds of expressions in the photos.

Anxiety or sorrow, so as I walked, I attached names to the wrinkled faces.
You are Anxiety, you are Sorrow, Sorrow then Anxiety, Anxiety, Sorrow, Sorrow.

My content, anxiety and sorrow, made from a lifetime of grunting and pigging out.
Sorrow and anxiety, *your call along the barley field's narrow path*. Pig passes by.

But Pig is told to drag out a pig from the inside of its heart and clean up its pigsty.
A monk passes by carrying a bamboo stick after hitting Pig who fell asleep while meditating.

Anyway, to nail Pig on a cross would be too natural, meaningless.
Anyway, if Pig dies and resurrects as Pig, what pig would believe it?
Anyway, I shouldn't have come here, a temple-stay doesn't suit me at all.

You know, I'm going to confess in a bit, but I'm Pig, I was originally Pig.

Pig Pigs Out

It's Pig, Pig who has never seen the outside, always Pig, depressed Pig, Pig who cries wolf, Pig who has chosen the most terrified pig in the world to be the king, Pig who shouts Oh, fantastic sewer! while hugging its pillow, Pig who laughs alone hoping mummy will get arrested, mummy who gave birth to Pig who will pig out till it drops dead, Pig with bloated lips who thinks the whole world is rice porridge, it's XXXL Pig, Pig who takes up the entire bed, its name can only be Pig, shivering-shivering Pig whenever it hears Cross the ocean, yes-yes Pig who has never once raised its head, Pig who pigs out from fear when it looks up at the vast night sky, Pig who pigs out thinking that Pig who pigs out is Pig

Droopy front and back limbs Pig, oinks with its tail tucked between its legs Pig, air is bundled up but why is it so heavy Pig, smells like a steaming cloud when you put your hand in its armpit Pig, unbelievably soft Pig, ultimately snuggly Pig, play all your life riding on me Pig, rats gnaw on piglets yet cosy Pig, what have you stuffed into your eyes Pig, why doesn't Pig know that it's Pig Pig, a photograph knows a mirror knows only you don't know Pig, never has looked out a window Pig, teeth pulled Pig, sigh Pig, regret Pig, after its teeth are pulled out and its tail cut off its tongue is lonely all by itself in its mouth Pig, but whenever it opens its mouth makes pig pig sounds Pig, pork Pig

qqqq   the sound of Pig crying along with a crow perched on its head
qqqq   naturally it's Pig screaming when its owner goes to jail and piss and shit rises up to Pig's knees
qqqq   the words that Pig yells inside when it denies being Pig
qqqq   the words that Pig utters You're Pig when you turn around to look at your mummy being taken away

qqqq   most of all, the squeals of our nation's pigs that don't know that I'm Pig

Your Imperial Majesty, Ferroconcrete!

Your Majesty, Four-walled Ferroconcrete!
Has your mood ever sucked?
Have you ever heard a cry for help?
(since everyone cries for help)
Why do you keep demanding that I discard myself?
Because I say my mood sucks? But you are not a psychiatrist

not even a police officer
Why do you keep making me feel as if I'm living in a piddly rented room
saying that the world only belongs to your descendants?
Why do you have me staring at the wall at the crack of dawn?
I want to go up on the roof and see the mountains below with a pair of binoculars
If not I want to have something more to eat from the kitchen
Why should I stare at the wall and discard myself
when my inner child only whines, pants, and never grows up?
Do I really exist so that I need to discard myself?
Your Majesty, Four-walled Ferroconcrete!
Is it all right to lift my hands up to my shoulders?
Please speak to me even if it's far more difficult to listen to you
than to look for my own shadow that's fallen into water
I know it's pointless to say You four walls! Attack me!
What the heck! The monk strikes my shoulder three times
with a bamboo stick

Feels like I'm Pig grunting in front of the wall
You're something else, sitting on a special cushion prepared by Fear
and Time tied up like a light bulb
drilling Pig to ditch Pig
I pull out the tissue stuffed in my back pocket as if it's an amulet
Your Majesty, Four-walled Ferroconcrete!
Every single grain of rice that I'll eat in the future is whirling about
My outsides hurt

Haven't you ever left your body?
Sir Four Walls have their arms on each other's shoulders
They sit me in the middle then
tell me not to get dragged by a Zen koan but to pull it along as I go
Where do you want me to go?
Who the hell are you?
Why do you write?
Are you saying you want to get killed right now?
Or are you telling me to die?
You jerk who lives on the suffering of others

I really can't meditate facing the wall
Talking with the wall doesn't agree with my constitution

Kitchen Confidential

The end of summer is always the kitchen of every house!

Women's hair scatters like luffa, the field where fat cows lie down beneath the children's eyeteeth is where bones are cracked opened – *how could I possibly forget this place?* That place where crimson cheeks are thinly minced and plunge into sugary boiling saliva, that place where the eyes of the deep ocean ripen like clusters of grapes – *how could I possibly?*

Woman inside an oyster shell
built a house as slippery as an oyster
The house quickly turned bad like an oyster
and was slippery-slippery to chew on

Things that came out of the house easily fractured
Its heart was good for splitting into four parts

So things would taste right for an open-mouthed cave
so water would spew up from the saliva pool
so a piglet inside a tummy would fall asleep

Mummy raised a baby inside her mouth
The baby lovingly gnawed on mummy
The baby ripened
Mummy! Where's the farthest place in the world?
I answered A place where there is nothing to eat!

Teeth lined up along the riverside and
the throat swallowed the sun
The river flowed whispering to my teeth
Don't swallow that bird
Don't chew that waterfowl

Plates-break   oil-splatter   soy-sauce-pours-out   I'm-tired my-wrist-gets-scalded   food-gets-stuck-to-a-frying-pan   burnt-outside-uncooked-inside apron-is-dirty   water's-cut-off   sewer's-back-up clothes-smell customers-return   glass-cups-are-murky   sugar-spills-out cigarette-ashes-spatter fish-scales-stick-to-my-hands   Voyager-explodes oil-catches-fire pot-is-soot-black knife-is-dull   revenue-and-health-department-officers-rush-over   food-scrap-sludge-overflows   turkey-in-the-oven-burns

The piglet keeps demanding Food, Food all day long

I know but the squeal-squeal always-hungry pig in my tummy doesn't know
That's the end of me
my adam's apple ready to decompose like a rotten oyster

A seagull pecks on its own fallen eyeball

Mummy's heart is scooped-scooped up like ice cream, tattered-tattered unthreaded
hands fall into the soup pot – *how could I possibly forget this place?* That place
where the moon scrapes-scrapes feeding on the western sky with a spoon and
its bones are simmered into a cloudy broth, that place where you drink the
juices of the corpses in the ground added to that broth – *how could I possibly
forget this place?*

Finally the end of autumn is always the kitchen of every house!

The place where teeth line up inside the boiling river beneath the blue knife

The Most Delicious You in the Whole World

Pigs walk on over
on this sunny afternoon
on this afternoon of flowers in bloom
Pig9 one-piece-dress-pig, Pig9 two-piece-dress-pig, Pig9 neck-tie-pig walk
shaking their buttocks side-to-side pock-pock in high heels

Pig9 Please raise and eat me
Pig9 Please cry after eating me
Pig9 I'll give birth to piglets
Pig9 Please say for once that you had a sad life
Pig9 Please wrap me up well and prepare me for a meal
Pig9 Please hang my intestines on a string
Pig9 Please don't throw away any part of me
Pig9 Please don't burp so loudly

May I call this delicious thing You?

May I gently-gently lovingly gnaw on you?

You love pigs
You skilfully cut out the flesh, wrap it in newspaper, then bag it in black plastic

Pigs all have the same name

Pigs walk on over
I've eaten them all yet they keep walking
I'm so stuffed yet they walk again

Pig9 lies down, its nipples on top of shit
Pig9 lies down, its nipples on top of shit

The Order of Cooking

1

I'm Pig
an exhibitionist pig patient

I divvy up my feces with my readers

Try touching it, there's nothing softer than this

Please hang up what I've written in the air like Pig

as you would hang a fat dictator in the square

2

The dead one comes and strikes the one that killed
The dead one offers dinner before it strikes the one that killed
Eat sweet things first
Eat before the aroma dissipates
Eat till you're stuffed
Offers just the right amount
Then it's the dead one's turn to cook the one that killed
in sync with the music from a radio someone turned on
on the opposite side of Earth

When tanginess swirls in my mouth the tanginess drains out from the night sky
of a foreign country
When mounds of sweetness rise in my mouth sweetness vanishes from the dusk
When the smell of coffee mushrooms in my mouth an unknown face
strides–strides into me toting an unknown weapon

Valentine's Day stars linger sourly in the dark blue night sky as the silver foil peels off
The face of the new grave ripens like the face of a girl

I am someone who cooks at home
I place a knife on the cutting board and cover my eyes
I pray for the dead, for their bliss

My turn to be eaten has arrived

Dear Pig, From Pig

Some day in the future, we are shooting a documentary. We are in the middle of filming an organ farm project that will provide organs for an ego that will live forever. I'm the most beautiful actress in the cast. This thought helps me a great deal with my acting. I'm raised to be your heart. I'm raised to be your lungs. I'm raised to be your skin. I'm raised to be your gall bladder. Furthermore, I'm raised to be your brain. That is to say, I keep an eye on you then quickly swap your eyes with mine. As I smile, I quickly switch your liver with my fresh liver. You never die since you replace your organs endlessly. In other words, it helps tremendously, in this line of work, that I'm a beautiful actress. I'm raised to be your sorrow, your tears, your anxiety, your fear, your defect. At times I've asked you Do you want to be the most bored person in the world without me? But you raise me to have me become you. Yes, yes, Master. I imagine that day when my heart goes to greet you, the day when I become you completely. But as lumpy flesh, would I be able to recognise my face? You come wearing a green fluorescent vest and tie my limbs to drag me. You are my liver, you are my kidneys, you are my heart, you are my eyes, you are my skin, no matter how much I wail, you drag me away not knowing that I am you. You occasionally shove a wooden club into me as you drag me. You need to be jailed for pig surveillance blasphemy embezzlement torture threat. You say You cancer-ridden lump of meat as you shove me into a tiny sty.

Dark Giggle Club

Bodies filled with filthy water
Pigs oink-oink in the sty
Why, they all look alike!

A girl goes dancing after sorting her family's trash

Oh that fantastic-sewer-daddy hit me
Oh that water-filled-jar-mummy abandoned me

Daddy pig eats numbers and buttocks dangle from the cheeks of mummy pig

The filthiest thing in the world are
little swine who want to become mummy
sniffling little swine who want to become daddy

Daddy raises me to make me daddy
Mummy raises me to make me mummy

I'm shaking my body to brush off
the mummy-daddy smell stuck to my body

I'm filthy at the moment
My body spotted with mummy-daddy shadows is really dirty

Me me me me die but mummy and daddy live forever

Mummy is filthy like greasy clouds
Daddy is filthier as mucky water boils inside him

A gigantic black envelope opens up between the ground and the clouds
The night when the darkness carries us and dances wavering-wavering
Why, everyone's confession in the world is ultimately the same!

Dirty, dirty, mummy-daddy only shit out death
They are as filthy as the truck loaded with pigs

The night when I get sloshed at a jam-packed club

The night when a knife-blade from faraway, shining like a new moon, arrives
to cut out the shadows from my body

The night when I vomit while shaking the intestines that will become
mummy's or daddy's someday in the future

Pink Pig's Fluid

Pink you is floating away in the sky, the naked you
I love watching your naked body, so I clap my hands cha-cha-cha

A full-moon tray passes through your pink body
There is nothing in the world plump you can't digest
After the tray, the black Okhotsk umbrella passes through your body

Clouds are the same as you and your ancestors
Winds are the same as you and your descendants
(But I say it like this)
(Pink pig is floating away in the sky!)

In the middle of the wailing rainstorm striking the pigsty
Mummy pig has 8 nipples
but 9 piglets have survived
Mummy pig snaps-snaps off each nipple to boil up a dumpling soup
yet the ninth pig dies
Why does the prettiest thing in the world have to leave first?
Why does the worst smell in the world have to leave last?
like the smell of the dead piglet that won't separate itself from Mummy's
embrace

This time, the new moon mutilates your insides as it passes through
There is nothing in the world that you can't digest but
qq qqq the western sky turns crimson as you digest the knife-blade

yet I love yawning and stretching inside your pink body so much that
I totally forget who you are whose daughter you are whose mummy you are
I put shoes on all four paws and clap-clap clap-clap-clap my hands and feet
It's the hour when all the swimming pools in the world are overflowing with pink

There are so many pink you's floating about in the air that my sky is too
crowded

Pig-Zen

Why is it that I'm left only with the shadows of those who have departed?
Why is it that the word pig won't detach from me?

The room where all the sounds have been sucked up by a silent vacuum cleaner
The room where the leaves of a nameless tree caress a light-coloured curtain

We have to walk on tiptoe
Over the wall, a monk has lived an ascetic life in silence for 8 years
Every time the door through which the monk's meal comes in and out opens
the explosive stench stinks far more than a pigsty
Venerable monk! Venerable monk! Wall-staring monk! I have a question!
Have you gone without a bath for the past 8 years?
Have you heard of drifting-zen?
Icebox-drifting-zen floats away across the vast sea!
A fisherman in an icebox!
He hasn't had a sip of water for 8 days!
Venerable monk! Venerable monk! Wall-staring monk! Have you heard of this?
Solitary-confinement-zen! You get beat up and yelled at Fess up! Fess up!
in a room without a toilet for something you haven't done.
Anyhow, how about shit-zen?
Zen that stares all day long at the shit I've shat as it keeps shitting drip-drip
Trapped inside a coma-zen! Behind a barred window pig-zen!

I'm a pig that doesn't know that I'm Pig
But when I spill my face into the sink water I see Pig
I'm a teacher who doesn't know that I'm Pig
I only draw mucky water on the board
I'm a patient who has to comfort the pig inside me
and I see only sitting pigs inside people

What can I do with this animal that stinks when it skips a bath for just one day?
What can I do with this pig that squeals oink-oink when it's not fed for just
one day?

Venerable monk! Venerable monk! Wall-facing monk!
If you stare at the wall long enough does it open up?

When I go outside the wall it's as though I'm trapped by the outside
The boss, the judge, the general, the police chief, the detective, and God live
outside the wall
When the wall opens, an interrogation begins. Venerable monk! Venerable monk!
Wall-facing monk!
Are you seeing through me from behind the wall?
Are you listening to my confessions?
If so, please try putting pink flesh on top of the shadow
not on the schizophrenic tree leaning against the curtain
Please try hanging up a plump pink flower, I'm freezing

The room where the flies chew the disciples like gum
The room so quiet that milk spills out from my breasts when I hear a loud noise

I'm a pig that doesn't know that I'm Pig
I'm a fat woman, a headache
I'm a fat woman's shadow, vomit
I'm a black, oily bag without wings
I'm Pig that gnaws on my own body
The room where all the Buddhas of the world sit with their backs turned and
groan
I'm a rock with hairy armpits

Marilyn Monroe

Don't say that I lived in a world as pure as the movie screen
that I flew on a silver plane to go and
lie down on a bed as clean as the inside of a mirror
and put my hand on my forehead
that I lifted up my willowy willowy skirt

We return as pigs
We snap back onto the pig magnet that eats and shits

Don't say that I pinned a flower in my hair
lay down on my icy death bed
inserted oxygen tubes and buzzed-buzzed frigidly cold
We return as hot pigs
We return for our final act
The act in which our fingers rot even before we lie down in our coffins

Don't say that you and I made q q sound roused by the fireworks
that left no ashes even when they burned burned
that we hatched like white butterflies at the cliff's edge
the sound of a puddle inside our body splash-splash
but that it all sounded slightly different
that we washed our outer body with water daily
and washed our inner body with blood
Dirt collects between our toes
and a box sealed up by sleep gives off a stench

Therefore I stick to the final act
The act in which I shit out my body, splash on top of what I have shat
The act in which my soul escapes then I'm hooked on a metal hook
The act in which I can taste my own tongue as I get mashed up

The woman carrying in each hand a bag of pig hearts
keeps walking and mumbling the same story

One drop two drops of urine-like rain are falling

Lips Stuck to a Landmine

Oh there goes a filthy bitch
there she goes after she's been beat up
Oh there goes a dazzling damned bitch
running away
Oh there goes a bitch shiny-black like a sewer
taking off

People with whips swarm in Stop the bitch!

I want to live alone
The discarded bitch
pig-like bitch
runs off

This is all because of the water in the dirty sack
she cries

I also don't like the sack filled with this water
she drools

Someone embraces Pig then slaps its cheeks
This filthy pig makes me mad, filthy woman

Filthy filthy filthy I'm so filthy
I should just live in my dream, why did I come here?

Die, Pig!
Why do you suck on milk?
Why do you grow up?

I wouldn't if I were you
Master comes and feels how thick your fingers have become
how your flesh has plumped up
I wouldn't grow up if I were you

Oh there goes beloved Pig
It's chased out

Oh one woman is trying to come out from Pig

Don't touch don't touch don't touch Pig anymore

Halved black Pig
There goes a shadow hanging onto her

Bloom, Pig!

Has to die even if it didn't steal
Has to die even if it didn't kill
Without a trial
Without a whipping
Has to go into the pit to be buried

Black forklifts crowd in
No time to say Kill! Kill!
No time for the blood to splatter onto the shit-smeared walls or light bulbs
No time for the piglets just popped out from the stomach to get skinned and
made into cheap colourful shoes

No time for the pale-faced interrogator wearing dark sunglasses to yell Fess
up! Fess up!
No time to gamble with terror as if skipping rope, whether I can survive the
torture or not
No time to bite the flesh of my mouth as if biting the hand that's hitting my
friend's cheek in the next room
No time to tie up hands and feet and pull my head back and force water into me
No time to say Mummy please forgive me, I was wrong, I won't do it again
No time to put a towel over my face and pour water from a pot
No handcuff or strap

Every night I read my country's history of torture
Then in the morning I open the window and sing loudly at the roofs below the mountain
How could I possibly forget this place?
I have Pig who needs to be rinsed with a song then go
Dear Song, Please stay stuck to my body for 12 hours

A horde of healthy pigs like young strong men get thrown into the pit

They cry in the grave
They cry standing on two legs, not four
They cry with dirt over their heads
It's not that I can't stand the pain!
It's the shame!
Inside the grave, stomachs fill with broth, broth and gas

Stomachs burst inside the grave

They boil up like a crummy stew
Blood flows out the grave
On a rainy night fishy-smelling pig ghosts flash flash
Busted intestine tunnel their way up from the grave and soar above the mound
A resurrection! Intestine is alive! Like a snake!

Bloom, Pig!
Fly, Pig!

Boars come and tear into the pigs
A flock of eagles comes and tears into the pigs

Night of internal organs raining down from the sky!
Night of flashing decapitated pigs!
Fearful night, unable to discard Pig even if I die and die again!
Night filled with pig squeals from all over!

Night of screams, I'm Pig! Pig!

Night when pigs bloom dangling-dangling from the pig-tree

Netherworld Waltz

The time when I was with flesh
flesh was me
even though I've never been inside it
I was startled when flesh touched the hot flame
In bed I hid my breasts under the sheets
for it's embarrassing to be defenseless
the room inside flesh
I sprayed tranquillisers stimulants antidepressants
anticonvulsants to catch a bug

I look back as I leave
On Pig's back a sack of me, cloud-like
carrying the fickle shadow, jockey-like
Pig's legs finally gave out after spilling dark sweat
Not the best fitting tailored suit for me but
it shed ten-fingered flesh gloves and ten-toed flesh socks
On top of them tiny windows, fingernails and toenails
Someone's looking out the window

Waking pill
Sleeping pill
Outing pill
Vomiting pill
Pill induced pill vomiting pill

I wrap the fallen thing that's like a dead exclamation mark in white cloth and
leave it behind

firmly believing the thing shedding that thing and roaming is me once again

Going to the Gate of Temple

I'm told to discard my body and go but I take it with me
I'm told to discard Pig and go but I take Pig with me

Leave the dream
I'm told just to become a bird
but a bird cries inside me

Time to say goodbye, I can live without you

111

Pig follows me

I'm that woman
that hideous, filthy woman
that woman, her stomach full of oblivion
that woman, her head filled with vomit
that woman, the girl passing by spits at
that woman, everyone runs away from when she stands at the street corner
squirming beneath the rubber boots of scary men
doesn't know how to dodge, for the house of letters is so small
her face smudged with dirt, her dirty buttocks, her blood-stained toenails
I'm that woman, can tell from miles away the sound of the funeral car coming
for me
that woman, eats out of fear, screams out of fear, eats out of fear again
that woman, eats what's been vomited, eats what's been shat – I'm a rice pot
stuck onto lips
repulsive woman, smelly woman, crazy bitch, smacked bitch
If I lie on a plate, will you brush tasty sauce on me and grill me?
I'm that ugly woman, takes a slew of antibiotics every day
You say you'll love me, sympathise with me but
I'm Pig

To add a bit more, I'm a fun pig
I look like this secret, I'm about to burst with humour
I'm a bladder that children can kick around in the schoolyard

Pig follows me keeping its distance as I head towards the temple gate
It's cold after being in a 36.5 degree Celsius room. Pig brings a stinky coat
and follows.

Joy to the world, the Pig is come
Let earth receive her Queen!

Dear Choly, From Melan

In November I was sleepless
In November the stars on the ceiling all lit up
In November my heart was so bright that I couldn't close my eyes
I was in a precarious state as the cold well rose above my head
Melan and Choly lay in a blue bucket, making fists
They clammed up like a cavity-ridden piano

Melan covered herself with a cloud, Choly with a shadow
Melan endured the wind, Choly clung to the sea
Melan said It's flesh-scented, Choly said It's water-scented
Melan disliked sunlight, Choly's feet were cold
Melan didn't eat, Choly didn't drink
I was absent when Melan ate, also when Choly drank water
Melan is a Frag, Choly is a Ment
Melan is a Dis, Choly is a Perse
My skin cracked like a jigsaw puzzle
Melan said Long ago, Choly wept ages ago
Melan ate soap, Choly became laundry
I swirled the wet laundry around my neck like one of Saturn's rings
Melan has a tongue of ice, Choly has eyes of ice
My shoulders hurt from carrying ice

A woman appeared with a yoke loaded with
Melan on her left shoulder, Choly on her right
Heaven hell, heaven hell, continually binary
like a Tibetan grandma's spinning prayer wheels
The woman poured beneath my skin a bucketful of Melan then Choly
and left

Kim Su-yŏng is Kim Su-000
Kim Ch'un-su is Kim Ch'un-###
Kim Chong-sam is Kim Chong-333
Step left then step right
After 0 is 1, after 2 is 3
After Melan is Choly

A night when all the mathematics of the world appear
The poets I admire are still clinging to death's umbilical cord

Dear Melan, from Choly
Dear November, from December

Melan combed rain streaks, Choly ploughed them
Melan put a white running shoe on her left foot
Choly put a white running shoe on her right foot
I covered up a pair of white birds, strings cut, on my feet

I couldn't come and go as such

NOTE: Kim Su-yông, Kim Ch'un-su, and Kim Chong-sam are the names of prominent contemporary male Korean poets who are all deceased. The last syllables of their names 'yông', 'su', and 'sam' are treated as homonyms for numbers.

Glasses Say

I keep my eyes open, for I'm a pair of eyeglasses.
I have never seen anything, for I'm just the glasses.
I remain still like a fan shell on a grill, not staring at anything,
especially since I don't know how to close my eyes.
I'm like Time eating ice.
After I'm done, I don't know what I ate.
It's similar to the way sand gnaws on waves,
for more waves swarm in again.
I don't see, feel, or think.
I'm colourless.
There is ocean in my left eye
and sky in my right. That's all.
In between the sky and ocean there's me. That's all.
I'm like a wooden raft moored by the seaside, drifting back and forth.
Don't ask where I'll be in ten years.
I'll just be, for I'm the glasses.
I might be lying down with my legs crossed.
I'll just be whether I'm put on or not.
Someone coming towards me divides into two scenes,
sky to the left and ocean to the right.
So speaking to the glasses is nonsense.
It's the same as speaking into their ears.
To say such and such about our memories in front of me is the most
nonsensical of all nonsense.
That doesn't mean that I'm hard of seeing, glazed over in white
I'm just here with my eyes open. Vacantly – it's such a great word.
Are you vacant? I'm vacant.
There is a lady diver.
She dives into the sea to find fan shells, a 25-metre oxygen tube tied to her
diving suit and wearing a helmet like an astronaut's.
She walks around in the deep sea eight hours a day.
Every three hours, she comes up to the boat and drinks milk, eats bread.
She searches through the sand again.
She looks like a black seal with its neck tied to a rope. Her slippery skin.
Fan shells are hidden beneath the sandy desert of the deep sea.
A vacant place. Only fan shells, a hook, an oxygen tube, a pair of goggles.
And a lady behind the goggles.
I shave a large piece of ice to make lenses.
I put the lenses in my mouth.
It's raining in the sea.

The sea says.
I keep my eyes open,
for I'm a pair of glasses.

Horizon Scratch

I open a black umbrella beneath the bare branches
for the sky seems torn

I open a black umbrella when you frown
for everything around me is like a broken mirror

I open a black umbrella under your hair
for I'm wearing a hat that's been shredded a thousand, ten thousand times

I open a black umbrella under the broken mirror
for I need to hold up my shattered self

I open a black umbrella when your nerves all stand up blue
for the wet blue second hands spill out

I open a black umbrella when plankton descend like fog
for I'm hungry even if I eat and eat

When a lit-up train goes by in the distance
When your spit splatters onto my face
When my younger sibling keeps vomiting in a faraway place

When I suddenly want to buy a black piano and set it under the radiant sun
When inside my dream someone shreds a black cloud to bits
while uncoiled mattress springs jab me

When my body begins to tremble uncontrollably
white paper opens a white umbrella
for my dirty writings are about to fall

Ghost School

I work at a ghost school
In this neighbourhood if you've been a ghost for over ten years you automatically
become an institutional ghost
I teach a class to the newly enrolled ghosts
(It's really impossible to disappear because of this work)
First, I have them carry a book on their heads and practise walking without
touching the ground
No one listens to what I say and there is no place to stand or lie down
I make them practise so they won't be shocked even if they leave no footprints on
the snowfield
I make them practise falling asleep floating in air
I teach them such things as how to overcome melancholy inside a coffin
how not to spew out hot air in the basement morgue
how not to turn into mummies even when a desert drags them away
I don't know myself, but I just say whatever comes out of my mouth
how to use a telescope or microscope made in the Time factory
how to have an out-of-body experience
how not to despair even when they become forgotten souls or when echoes don't
return
how to wish that they could set something ablaze
how to rage into you as bright as the fireworks lingering in the night sky
can be found in the textbook, but I'm not writing it
how to sob hiding inside a song
how to hold their breath hiding inside the sobbing
how to flow with the flowing people then spur themselves up to the sky sobbing
like a tree
how to erase my body's margins and become an adjective
as the sounds from a brass instrument navigate like planes taking off
and therefore how each day becomes fainter
are all in the magic that has been passed down
then I add
a ghost that takes revenge is low rank
a ghost that only appears in a night of sleet is middle rank
a rotten ghost luring a swarm of flies is high rank
a ghost that is like a cloud, a question, gas is high-high rank
and high-high-high rank, etcetera, which nobody knows about
All right then, shall we practise raging like spring snow
as if pulling out the left wing first from the body where swarms of flies have died?
Then I issue a warning to the ghosts who haven't done their homework
Damn! You can only become institutional ghosts after graduating from a ghost school

Cloud's Nostalgia

Rabbit's ear entered as the white wall laughed
I pulled that smelly thing
Rabbit-cloud mushroomed

Buttocks-cloud came down from the ceiling
Those buttocks belong to the wrestler at our neighbourhood gym

A rope for strangling came down, but it dispersed as soon as it hanged a neck
The walls floated in air and barked
The door opened to the room where the angels were tortured and had cried
My screams poured out like shit, so I opened an umbrella to receive them

A thousand nipples protruded from my body
Every nipple needed to be milked white milk
My body overflowing with milk was swollen like a jar
The jar smelled of white rabbit

Those plastic things, paper, cloths
In my room I sang about the memories of my attachment to those things

When I sang, all the sweat pores on my body salivated
my black fur got wet

I pulled the mask tightly like a shoestring
and waddled out like a wrestler

Now it's time to confess, my lover is that cloud
Water falls from its face every time its expression changes hundreds of times a day

Shall I call it The sleep of someone who has left?
(I almost said A dirty sight, for I'm unable to forget it)
Shall I say It's a flustered rabbit because its hutch has vanished?
Shall I say It's melancholy's nostalgia?
Or shall I say Your facial expressions fall off every second and get buried in the
ground?

Green-strawberry-summit-cloud
White-hair-cloud encircles god's neck
Hook-cloud hooks my neck's artery onto a cloud
Lens-cloud opens the lid of my house and peers into it

Over there, the boys from martial arts gym run into the sunset with red briefs over their heads and

I pull threads from the crimson cloud and weave my undergarments and twist my fat fattened body

The Way Mummy Bear Eats a Swarm of Fire Ants

that my body grows uncontrollably large
that every time a wound appears I cut up a small piece of cloth to cover it
cut up and cover, cover again then
find myself covered with a quilt pulled over my head
my mummy told me never get under a quilt
never learn to quilt
she told me as I patch and patch I'll never get out of poverty
that now I'm walking like a bundled up garbage quilt
that at one point you used to eat me bite me control me
use me but now I've become a quiet
thing like a bundle of garbage
that I smell like a homeless person who has become one with a pull cart
that when kicked lightly by front hoofs, I'm like a deer, roe deer
that I'm huge to the point of dying
that there is only me on the freeway scorched by sun
that there are only things that run away when they see me
like the enormous gray bear that sleeps while it walks
like the enormous black lace cloud fluttering above eyelids
like the dump truck leaking dribbles of oil in the middle of a desert
like the house with rotten stairs and six feet of dust collected in the attic
that there is no one except me standing all alone
that I'm getting larger and larger
as I'm chased, chased off the road
that I'm filled with all the screams of the world
that there is nothing else but that

Wound's Shoes

I shove my feet into the wound
I go around wearing the wound
Or maybe the wound gets around, carrying smelly shoes
The wound is a pus mould made just for me

Shoes made of wound have flowers all over
When I shove my feet in the shoes, dark-pink globules are crushed
Shoes made of wound are a chicken's throat, a chicken with its belly cut open
When I shove my feet in, small rib bones break off
Shoes made of wound are an open grave
When I shove my feet in, my left foot my right foot
have on mummy's and daddy's graves

Wound's shoes get hysterical at times, but they are patient overall
Blisters burst and rotten stench mushrooms
They bite down on my filthy feet, their pink lips tightly shut
My feet don't know whether the shoes are in pain or not

Wound's shoes have no sense of direction
Over there is always here and here is over there
Wound's shoes insist that every place I step is here
Whatever wound's shoes step on, that's my spot for the moment
When the shoes become huge the feet become huge too
I wear shoes that have become as big as a hot rice sack
and jump like a white pig running away with its belly cut open

Shoes made of wound are full of rice
I shove my feet into the pot of perfectly cooked rice
Rice gets crushed like tiny roe under my feet
Shoes made of wound are mummy's sagging breasts
When the shoes touch the ground, they leave milky tear marks!
The sensation of shoving my stinky toes into someone's warm throat that has
swarms of flies stuck to it

Right now, I'm walking in the scorching sun, wearing wounds slanted outwards

Birthday

When I open my eyes in the morning
my bed is full of thorns
When I listen to music
thorns spill out from the speakers
When I walk
thorns pile up beneath my feet
I must have become a watch
Pointed second hands
protrude from my body
They needle me, saying
You poor thing
You poor thing
I walk through the second hands raining down at night
till I'm one hundred, two hundred years old

Over there faraway
so remote that the place shines out
that you and I live there
that we are very happy
I send you my regards
on your birthday
with cake and candles
made from those second hands

The Salt Dress Inside Me

When sorrow is endured, salt gets excreted from your body
Your salty-salty expression
Your animal gaze
like a lonely island hammered by the sea

Some days when there is a high-sea warning
seawater gushes in over the short eyelash fences
but the salt's architecture doesn't crumble
salt-flowers bloom from my fingertips like stinging sobs

Salt, turns my fallen shadow into powder and scatters it under the streetlamps
Salt, persists in me like the sea's architecture

Salt, we embrace tightly and try
to capture the sea in each other

The salt pond is at work as soon as I'm awake
I listen to the rising sea architecture

I am wearing the salt dress
inside me

Key

Your appearance from behind, distanced in the backlight, is a keyhole
Inside the hole is the outside world

The ridge of a dark mountain zigzags like a key's blade
I want to hold the ridge in my hand and open you

That faraway place, the poor shimmering meadow
dangles behind the keyhole
so I pinned an armful of lilies onto the meadow but

click

It's written in the books the dead read
that all our bodies are the door that opens the path of light

but why do you open me then go alone?

The keyhole you left on before you vanished

The darker-than-night-pitch-black-naked-body you left on
by boring a hole on the last day of the waning moon

The meadow filled with fragrance of the lilies grows remote inside the hole

The Poetry Book's Open Window

There is a hundred-year-old hotel called Cheshire Inn
across from the Washington University in Saint Louis
and as in a fairy tale the Cheshire Cat lives in the hotel
While I was watching *Up In The Air* in my room
George Clooney entered a pitch-dark theatre
and jumped up like the Cheshire Cat

From here to a faraway place
Up In The Air

A pencil writes a poem with a shadow
and a candle writes with light

I decided to throw my soul, as black as soot, at the divinely
burning rods of the wall heater and rest for a bit
I thought to myself, I should cleanse my memories
since I've travelled to a far-off country
After my rest, I squeezed out sorrowtoothpaste
and brushed my teeth

The hotel where the mute ghosts come out and roam
As I lie down on the bed, page 45, layered with the shadows of the hotel guests
the cat that flowed out from the endless fairy tale
quietly passed by me and
one by one the fixtures in the room were erased
The powder of erased things piled up inside the cast iron stove
God quietly burned up in the chimney

My comb called mirror and mirror called light and light called me
Locked inside my sad eyes locked inside the mirror locked inside the room, I
put on mirrorcream and get slowly erased

Inside the cold flames of the wall heater
My face reflected faintly in the mirror, I asked the passing cat,
That face etched onto the glass is worth something, right?

The room knit tightly with fishing net
therefore without entrance or exit
The room where the ghosts appear in the mirror on time

(I sent a letter saying,
I'm now staying in a room of loss
so don't tell me to do my work or remember things
Don't take away my loss)

In the hallway, the paintings with life in them
gently swayed the tree roots inside the picture frames
and the wooden floor beneath my feet was slippery
as though on electric rollers
Darkness hung like a bright lamp and erased the hallway and the rooms
The hotel you have to depart from once again for the place you've left
even if you only take a single step forward

(After walking, then riding in the car
I stayed in that hotel. I even filled out a registration card
in my sleep and asked the housekeeper,
What's that lonely moon doing tonight?
He answered, It smears cream onto a face that's been erased)

Saturn's Sleeping Pill

A place where my shadows visit when I close my eyes
There, I put on a belt made of smoke
When my soul buzzes like the mosquitoes at night
my shadows swarm like a pride of lions on the plains
A place where my ashes get up and dance after I've been burnt today

Saturn has 60 moons
therefore, I have 60 shadows
I have 120 eyes, of course
I don't get to open all of my eyes
whether the sun rises or not

Therefore, how many bodies do I have?
How many more bodies can die?
The ground is soft-soft and my footsteps are limp-limp
The air is sticky-sticky and my heart heaves-heaves
A place where your ghost snatches my soul away like a spider web

I pray for my own soul
I sit on my dead bodies
and put to sleep a few remaining live bodies
Longings are asleep doubts are asleep
even the throats that have not yet opened are asleep all asleep

What do you want to be when you die?
I'm going to be something that has no borders

A place where the moons rise continuously continuously
A place where teeth poke-poke out
even if you press them down with a thick blanket
A place where the dark sooty lions perch on the faint horizon
their eyelids keep keep falling on the glowing rays from their eyes
When you part with the shadows there
you also part with the weight of my body here

Eyelashes

The body that has been soaking in shallow water for a long time must be hatching
Milky breaths bubble up non-stop

Soon, a pair of eyelids that has submerged the body in darkness soars

A hinged yellow door flies away
A ripple is scooped up with a skipping stone

It breathes, fluttering

I'm in a deep sleep, so the yellow butterfly is afar

The yellow powder that spouts from my mouth after I eat
a sticky rice cake covered in powdered soy
Rutting pine trees spurt pollen on the foot of the mountain

That thing as yellow as my molar tooth is flying away in the sun
It flies throbbing like the wind's hair

I write that my soul smells
I write that I want to spit out the throbbing yellow

The horizon is tied to the legs of the yellow butterfly
Thousands of whipping sticks stand up by the lake

The whirlwind of sleep and waking
blinks-blinks
I bite on the slanted line drawn between night and day
blink-blink

The horizon is dragged away, wound tight around my calves
The thing that submerged me was just those two clumps of hair

The pair of eyelashes is flying away all by itself across the lake
leaving its body somewhere behind

Morning Greetings

It's the hour when the sisters get up
and put on their black outfits
on top of their white blouses
Today I heard the bicycles tied up in front of the subway station
fall down all at once

Having to greet each other in the morning is an unstated law
Hello Dear Shadow who licked me all night long
Hello Dear Daddy inside my flesh who woke up when I did
Hello Dear Daddy who burned my guitar
Hello Dear Furnace who conducted my flaming guitar
Hello My Little Siblings who cried next to it
Hello Dear Father who told me that time will come to a stop
The same as above
but if I keep going for a bit more
Hello Dear Critic who folded my poems into paper boats and let them float in
dirty water
Hello Dear You – your ear holes become a hose as we talk
Hello Dear God the plumber – all of our hoses, yours and mine, are his
Hello Tattoo Needle that etches alone
The sky is throwing down clear bottles, Hello Dear Breaking Bottles, Hello
Dear Sprinkling Light
Shit, hurl like the shiny pride inside your head! Ball, throw! Water, spray!
Hellohellohello

The morning when I feel like saying goodbye to everything

I'm a soldier of goodbye
I'm a body that produced a dead infant
I'm a minus producing machine
If you get too close to me anyone turns into Minussoandso
I don't know why my music only subtracts and doesn't know how to add
I get carried away by music and disappear into the supersonic

In this country no one can choose the fall
Here people swarm all over to cure you
but I'll live together with the fallen angel for the time being

The place where I can't name myself, hello!
The place where I can't name my disease, hello!
Next morning I'll be born as a new illness
I'll pin myself onto the new illness
So hello everyone!
Dear You who have become Minus You, hello!

It's the hour when the ghosts that have stayed up all night
drape a black cape over my poor shadow
I heard the subway station weeping in sorrow, its first train not yet arrived

Influenza

When I pronounce 'bird'
only the wind remains in me
as if water, fire, earth all vanish
Maybe the name 'bird' is the illness of the name 'bird'
The bird makes the sound of blowing wind from my dripstone-like bones

We received an order to kill all the birds that couldn't fly
Since there was no time to kill, we received an order to put them in a sack
and bury them alive in a pit

A few days after I got married I placed a chick on a cutting board
and was about to strike the plucked bird with a knife
It felt as if I were holding the legs of a just-born infant
the chick covered in goose bumps was trembling
I wanted to wrap the bird in a baby's quilt and hold it in my arms

That thing that snoozes with its head pillowed on its chest
Have we really reached the end?
The nightmare's curtain rips and Death is born inside

Like a wall of wind my heart trembles to the rhythm

In my village now there are no such things with wings on them
They have all been put in the ground, powdered with disinfectant
My aunt was caught by Mr Gas Mask
when she tried to wrap her goose in a baby blanket onto her back

The fact that I'm writing a bird poem means
that I'm ill with the bird
A bird perched on my collarbone
pecks me
They say when you die you go with the wind
but now I go with the wind of the bird

As if all the kite strings of my country have tangled and piled up high in the sky
the white-feathered mountain flutters in the wind
and inside it 3-month old, 6-month old tiny eyes
heaped in layers
a few hours before they are shoved into the pit
they tremble with their eyes opened

God's Obsession Regarding Cross-Stitch and Lace 1.

You can get to know God's obsession regarding cross-stitch and lace
by leafing through an old pattern book where sun rises moon rises

You can also get to know about it naturally as you stand still by a riverside where
mist is falling

When you wrap the thin and transparent thread around your fingers for the first
time, you may be startled, Goodness it's so light
but this is how the long story, the faint lace begins
Will the lace grow up to be a bloodied undergarment?
or a bridal veil floating away in the river?
or an outfit worn in the ground below?

Ah it's a really amazing pattern
but if you leaf through the worn-out pattern book
like the curtain of mummy's first wedding night
the story is all in the pattern

Inside the transparent patterns full of holes
January 1, December 18, December 25

God is a cross-stitch and lace obsessive-compulsive patient
He sits on the windowsill like a curtain and overhears all the secrets of the inside
and out, flapping about

The day when my nervous system gets entangled like fishing lines
and thrown into the wavering bottom like a wrecked ship

slash slash slash
current current current

scrape scrape scrape
streak streak streak

crack crack crack
scratch scratch

You can get to know God's obsession regarding cross-stitch and lace
right away when you see that the foot of the mountain across from my brother's
house where 2500 pigs have been buried alive is completely covered in snow

Like when the butterflies with the whitest threads in their mouths spew out from
the scrunched larvae of death

Eyelashes bore through the old pattern book and come flying spot spot
the snowflakes as white as the kiss of the eyelashes

Weightless patterns close their eyes and fall on the field breath breath breath
emitting holes like the smiles of a girl

Her Obsession Regarding Lace and Cross-Stitch

Girl is knitting a smile

Girl is knitting a yawn

The lace is getting longer
Unsweetened girl nobody wants
is knitting lace
as if she were swiftly writing what everyone knows how to write
Her heart is breaking
Girl eats and sleeps at a boarding house and works at a convenient store as a cashier
Pale girl
Girl is knitting a bridal veil with vapor from the humidifier
Girl is wearing a bridal veil
The lace with a hundred billion of holes embraces her
Girl is being buried by the lace
Girl who has become as white as the ripped comforter with its strewn filling
is inside the damp lace grave, her mouth filled with white foam
Girl with many smiles, girl with fluttering eyelashes lowered during a poetry
workshop
Pale girl who is like the young granny in the black and white photo
Yet the most common girl in winter
Stupid girl does not know that she is the girl nobody recognises
The most colourlesstastelessodourlessnamelessboundless girl in the world

Girl's bridal veil is flapping over the river
The winter's first tiny white millions of crosses fall from the sky above girl's bridal
veil
like at a wedding funeral procession

Mrs Everest's Breakfast

As the helicopter pulls up a huge corset from the bottom of the sea
the fat woman who used to live hidden in the sea
is automatically pulled up along with it
Her white face, her blue tendons
a face that has never been exposed to light

He sits her down on a chastity belt
She has her breakfast every morning tied to the dining room chair's
armrests that look like fallopian tubes

The continent slowly heaves up from the sea as it dislikes the saltiness
It has soared so high that clouds gather below its feet
The ocean still stays hidden in the many crannies of Mount Everest
Dead clams flake off
The fossils of blue whales float
Somewhere inside her body a huge salt fountain spouts

(I wonder where the river that begins deep inside me flows to)

She thinks that she is having her meal on the mountaintop
The air is thin Over I'm here alone Over
Out of breath Over but no one should come here Over

The desert below the dining chair gets bigger, bigger every day
Like a corset the desert constricts river's thighs
then the river disappears
When the river disappears people disappear
a village disappears a nation disappears
The sand of the riverbed is as soft as flour
She makes bread with that flour and spreads jam on the toast for breakfast
The dust-cloud mushrooms beneath the dining room chair

I often sit on the top of the Himalayas
and imagine that I'm having breakfast
looking down at the boundless depths of the ocean
as I swing my legs wildly
below the dining table, below the clouds made of white table cloth

136

Really Really

Soil – the thing that's not at the flowerhouse, really
Sky – the thing that's not at the birdhouse, really
Ocean – the thing that's not at the fishhouse, really

You know better than I do the thing that's not at my house, right?

My house shoves out rats, lice, and roaches
prostrates and mutters-mutters reciting something
My house shoves out weed, rain, and ghost's hair
flinches-flinches from the wind, ripping the stairs

What's inside the words A tall house?
The teeth of the fallen worker are inside it
What's inside the words A faraway house?
My aged mummy's palms stuck to the wall are inside it

What's inside the words A happy house?
The flashing demon's eyes are inside it
so terrifyingly soft that you can't make a fist

In God's house only Mr Verbs – live, die – live in it
In my house only Mr Pronouns – me, me, me, me – live in it
In nature's house only Mr Adjectives – scary, scary – live in it

Who who lives in the house with a deep dark spring?
The streaming groundwater awake like a snake lives in it

One day like when a lengthy novel ends incoherently
my family leaves this world and
flowers bloom
butterflies fly
night passes
spring arrives
Would you like to eat with me?
The house where the hammer lives inside the clock that never dies hammers
on time
I wonder how many houses I get to live in during my lifetime, then I forget
Later when I become a ghost
which house will I appear in the most?

My house – the words that I understood outside my dream
but can't understand inside the dream, really
My house – the words that I understood when we lived together
but can't understand after I'm dead, really, really
In my next life how would we, we mummydaddyolderbrotheryoungersister
recognise each other?

However, however the boat sinks and
the sailors can't keep their eyes closed as they sink into the ocean!

Their eyes that said, *We want to go home!*

Ostrich

Its body is tiny like an embryo yet its wings are extremely long
This terrible thing came looking for me
a thing that is like a cross between a camel and a waterfowl
that hates land, sky, or water came looking for me
Its feet appear rock-hard for walking in the desert but
it has bulging cheeks for catching fish

Am I an ostrich that doesn't know it's an ostrich?
My glasses keep slipping down
This thing came looking around with glasses on the bridge of his nose

Actually my body's filled with a foreign language
Not English, Chinese, Ratese, Whalese, or Elephantese
It's a language I've never heard of, it's noisy as the scorching sun

Actually my body's filled with insects
Not flies, mosquitoes, ants, worms, or centipedes
They look like something that just escaped after sweating from a dead body
You have to look at them with a magnifying glass, but you could say they're
like my heart that has dispersed like dust inside me, couldn't you?
(like an organism anxious to eat me up after I'm dead)

Overall you could say it looks like an ugly tree that has come up from the
floor, couldn't you?
Its look of surprise, the way it speaks chirp chirp like a bird
You could say it looks like a fowl that has lost its feet, floundering about,
fallen into a dream, couldn't you?
You could say it looks like a weed that has made its way up through the crack
in my torn heart, even bored through my black bra and grown so tall,
couldn't you?
Anyway, it looks confused as if it's sticking its head out of a tiny hole

It looks faraway even if it's standing right in front
It roams the hallway at night, for its wings are too heavy for flight
I said this before but its body is tiny, yet its wings stretch endlessly

It's done with living, yet the moment of dying is so long!
It occasionally lets out the terrible cry of a camel!

I even get up from sleep to look at this thing
It reeks but we are good friends
When I first saw this thing
I thought that it was like my eyelashes
trapped in my retina for the last time when I die
like a Christmas tree deserted years ago in a vacant house
its terrible pose that doesn't allow it to rub the dust from its eyes
like looking into a microbe that has nested inside your nostrils
with a magnifying glass as big as a house!

Attendance Book

That year when I was late twenty-six times
my teacher made me kneel on top of his desk
I tried my best to keep my legs together
so my menstrual blood wouldn't stain my teacher's desk
then suddenly a student monitor came in
and hit me in the head with the attendance book and said
Do you want to keep getting punished? Or flunk?
He spilled out lectures and threats
You won't be able to graduate even if you become ancient
You'll get your joints torn by the advancing shields of blackboards or get
crushed
You'll need to get your ears pierced since you were born a woman
You'll need to use shoulder pads and walk as if you are hammering the ground
The pain won't let you take in the breath that suddenly comes looking for you!
It's the first time you've heard of this, haven't you? You'll have to push out
the baby
or you'll abort it and become a sparrow with its head buried in the ground
You need surgery to remove that rude expression of yours
The day will come when you'll have to take a knife to your face
You'll never be able to leave the kitchen during your lifetime just as you'll
also never be able to leave the classroom
Melancholy will come find you and the World War 3 will begin
and dinosaurs will become extinct and there'll be a nuclear explosion
and the sand-dust cloud will blow in every spring
and most of all the fishnet inside your chest will fall ill
so it won't be able to let out the dirty air
You'll see all the toads of the world run amok
and you'll have to pick one of them and get married
I'm saying this out of concern for you
there is no school better than this on this earth
so do you want to be punished here forever? Or flunk?
You ask a good question! There's no better school than this even on Mars!
You need to be punished some more
If you have committed the same crime outside the school
you'd be tortured by the National Intelligence Service that is worse than Hell
Your head will be covered in a black plastic bag and hung to a flag pole
You idiot, the idiot who so willingly climbs on top of the desk
So do you want to keep getting punished or do your want your name
engraved in the attendance book for life?

I started school when I was seven years old, but I'm still in school, don't even know how much time has passed
Sometimes I feel as if
I've been crushed by hot concrete and am still plastered to the classroom wall

Black Brassiere

On a very very boring day
like a waterfowl with its lips buried in its chest
I wanted to taste my own breasts
those eyes that stay open inside the black eye patches

My breasts might taste like the lighthouse
on an island far away from the mainland
or the island's prison, the taste of solitary confinement!
or the underground catacomb

(like the exploding waterfall tied up tight-tight)

(like the wavering sea, its wrapping paper ripped open)

(as if my body is generating my eyes)

(like two baby waterfowls looking for feed on the hills by the sea)

I once saw a photograph of hundreds of mothers in a square
waiting for their sons' corpses
I wanted to undo all the hooks
on the backs of the mothers
The eyes on the breasts sobbed sobbed
their crying echoed throughout the square
Please don't leave me behind
I'm your mummy

The sound of the swollen eyes inside the eye patches
hitting the prison wall bam bam!

The eye patches look like somebody's hands
The hands wearing black gloves clutch two chicks in their hands!

The fish caught in the net should repent, have you heard of such a thing?
The lost chick should repent, have you heard of such a thing?

My black bra straps
are stretched out
like two streams of tears

(Now I want to row to some deep place
like someone rowing in the middle of the sea wearing an eye patch)

Morning

In the middle of my cooking, I sing a carol
– *Away in a manger, no crib for his bed*
– *The little Lord Jesus laid down His sweet head* –
when my song was about to go over the highest note
a pale face showed briefly outside the letter 'd'

The girl departs alone riding the yellow air current of the country of anaemia

I quizzed my grandmothers
How many hours in a day do you feel like you are a girl?
Or a grandmother? Which do you feel more?

The girl lets out shallow breaths from a disinfected first-class bed capsule

That dizzying place, glory in heaven, peace on earth
The girl rides in the front of a white paper plane
frequently used by the thinnest perfection in my life
She only rides the daybreak
Her face flies over my vacant face while I cook
as if she were flying over someone sleeping

The morning when all of the time that departed from her lined up to serve her
The cold shroud, the transparent face, the body as cold as a razorblade

As a representative of grandmothers my mother
is close to eighty years of age and she says that the girl keeps appearing
that the girl keeps appearing as she gets older
she takes my quiz laughing covering her mouth hee hee hee

as if she has just come of the bath
the round-round, sunken, pale girl
looks undecided whether to open the door and
get off from my mummy's retired plane or not

Do you know why Munch's girl
sits naked idly on bed?
When she woke up she realised that she had become a girl
Time, wrinkles, clothes have all gone somewhere else

144

Praise the Lord who is in a whitest of white manger
This morning I knelt before her
Ticklish fluttering, sweet knees arose
from my red grape-like heart
A serving of my broken egg!
Would you like it scrambled? An omelette?

I serve fresh morning
at twilight when sorrow soars before sunrise
to the nameless girl who asks
Mrs! Where have you been all this time?
to me who can't recognise my own face
to the cold-hearted girl sitting in the front row of my paper plane

A Cup of Water

    With the desperate glance of a cup of water

forge the body thin as a knife blade
shove it in
spit it out from smelly mouth
go with eyes closed trapped inside a camel's hump
become a squirmy spirit-like thing
after detaching from a rotten body
only wants to go, depart
can't endure anything that doesn't depart

    With the light of water that caresses the body

I slid down from a lukewarm face
I wet my fingers and flowed down
That's how the previous life of a cup of water got spilled

    Why do people have that look in their eyes like they want to leave their
bodies?

gulp down the cup with eyes closed
go inside the dark throat
say 'I'm not waiting to be born again'
as you swim inside
get kicked out as a burp
rise up mixed into nirvana or soul
finally hang onto the cloud's toes

the water hasn't found its boundary yet
is a cup like an eye

A cup of water knows everything about the insides of our body that we don't know

APPENDIX

Poetry or Letter to the Other of My Inside-Outside:

An interview with Kim Hyesoon from *list_Books from Korea* (Winter, 2013).
By Shin Hyông-ch'ôl. Shin is a South Korean literary critic.

SHIN: You have published ten volumes of poetry since your debut in 1979.

KIM: I never look at my previously published books. Whenever I see my poems cited somewhere, I feel awkward and embarrassed.

SHIN: In something I came across published abroad, you are introduced as 'a prominent woman poet who has received two awards named after poets Sô Jông-ju and Kim Su-yông, who are representative of pure poetry and engaged poetry, respectively'. I was thinking that it may come as a surprise to the readers abroad that one poet alone could traverse and dismantle these two opposing poetic trends.

KIM: It feels embarrassing and awkward to receive awards, but then it would be even more awkward to draw attention to myself by refusing them, so I end up accepting them. I think the debate about 'pure poetry' vs. 'engaged poetry' was inevitable and essential to Korean poetry. I think Kim Su-yông, is a poet who went beyond the confines of the structure that he was in. Who would have known that my wailings, in everyday language, would amplify so much? I may be someone who belongs to both sides, or I may be a dual national who doesn't belong anywhere.

SHIN: This term 'woman poet' shows up above. In your case, I think that term has rarely been used with a negative connotation, but still you must be tired of it. I wonder if your book of criticism, *To Write as a Woman: Lover, Patient, Poet, Me* (2002), represents a koan, the endless questions you ask and answer in your lifetime. I want to get your latest take on this, and also do you think categorising poets by gender is meaningful or meaningless within contemporary poetry, and in what way?

KIM: No one fails to ask me about the term 'woman poet.' And even if I'm not asked about it, I always insist that I'm a 'woman poet'. The consumer of poetry has put me in the category of woman, differentiating me, and so I howl that the inside of that category is the place of paradoxical poetry.

When I was younger, I was active in a feminist group called Another Culture, and I observed then that the ideology of the women's liberation movement was in conflict with my poetry. In my everyday life and in my essay writing, I was engaged in feminist thought and activism, but my poetry covered my contentions with a sheath that was bright and alive, like something woven with vapour. Not only 'woman' became blurry, but also 'me' – this blurry state of being is poetry. My poetry tells me to bring the life-giving water that will save father's life as the songs of a woman heading to the afterworld, my poetry tells me to become a ghost.

When I was writing *To Write as a Woman*, I wanted to say that the ignition point of a genre called poetry is a 'feminine position.' I wanted to say, regardless of a poet's gender, poetry is where night is, where absence is, poetry begins where mother is (who has lost herself to me), it's where I 'do poetry.'

SHIN: Poetry differs from prose, so I think that in many cases the subject matter, imagination, and speech may occur simultaneously. I would like to ask about these three in the order above. What is the main 'passage' through which the things that are perceived as 'poetic' come to flow into your body?

KIM: The ignition point for poetry is multiple, but the material for ignition is one. My body has to be in a poetic state. No matter how great my ethical or feminist rage may be, no matter how much another text resonates with me, no matter if some dream smacks me and takes off, unless my body, the material for ignition, is in a poetic state, it is pointless. I am coloured by the poetic state like some kind of bodily sign. As if I'm about to cry, as if my laughter is about to explode in giggles, I need to overlap with a blank paper-thin girl. And while I write, the girl becomes a witch or grandmother, but first I need to be in that state. I call it the 'the state of something yet nothing'.

SHIN: Much of Korea's poetry is neatly written, depicting everyday experience along with an adequate message, yet your poetic texts provide inspiration to critics who are trying to theorise the role imagination plays in poetry. In your poetry there is fairytale-like imagination, grotesque imagination, mythical imagination and so forth; in fact, there are multiple imaginations at play.

KIM: When I began writing in my twenties, I just wrote down any 'poetic' thing that soared up in me. I wasn't conscious of what I was writing or why I was writing it. Back then I didn't even have friends or teachers. Meanwhile my imagination developed like the muscles of someone who exercises. Imagination is the process of moving muscle in sync with bone, to a place of freedom, poetry's vast outer side. It activates something to nothing. Perhaps I should say it's a cloud mill? The place where cloud(poetry) knows but poet(me) doesn't know. With bone and muscle, I repeatedly call someone who disappears into the slippery crack of time and space, someone who becomes more unfamiliar and mysterious by the day. Lately I've been thinking that someone laid up in an intensive care unit, or 'me' the woman, a few seconds before death, is dreaming for real 'now, here, me'. You could say it feels like the observed and the observer, before they perish, are trying to move something together, inflating the muscle of the ignition point.

SHIN: In the past, as well as now, whenever I read your poems, the first thing

150

that strikes me is the sense of liveliness and liberation of your speech. What kind of relationship is there for you between what you will say and how you will say?

KIM: Language is conversation, so poetry also converses with someone. Of course, that someone is not tangible or definable, someone on other side of cognition. That someone is preferably a poetic inspiration or poetic other. Naturally, speech begins directed at the other. Like illness, which is a reply sent by the body, poetry is also a reply in regard to inspiration or the other. Therefore, language or speech changes according to the one who is receiving the letter. And so each poem can only be spoken in a particular way, while striving first for the impossible communication with the other, rather than communication with the reader.

SHIN: In connection to the previous question, as a poet who writes in Korean, what kind of freedom does Korean allow for you, and, conversely, what structural aspects of Korean are suffocating to you and when do they occur?

KIM: When I write, I start to feel through my body that Korean has a 'feminine language' and a 'masculine language'. When I begin to write, in whichever language, it feels as if I'm tugging down on my skirt in an uncomfortable seat. It's not just the Korean language, for I also simultaneously feel the suffocation and freedom in regards to Korean poetry. Adding an aphorism after describing something is the way Korean poetry speaks, something which has been continuously passed down from when Korean poetry was written in the style of classical Chinese poetry and traditional Korean *sijo* [three line poem]. Maybe this is why I have extreme reservations about any explanatory statements in poetry. The Korean language has countless variations in adverb, adjective word endings, multiple onomatopoeias and mimetic words, and through them the Korean language is vibrant with ironies and fluid in syntax. And it's a phonetic language rich in history, which allows for possibilities of rhyming through countless homonyms that are closely or directly related. In translation, it becomes difficult to reveal all these aspects of wordplays in Korean.

SHIN: You have two books published in English translation. The selected poems, *Mommy Must Be a Fountain of Feathers* came out in 2008 and the collection of recent work, *All the Garbage of the World, Unite!* in 2011. Please introduce me to any new criticism of your work that you haven't encountered in Korea.

KIM: Johannes Goransson has used the term 'gurlesque' to review my poetry. Perhaps he has heard my 'girl's language'. I found it interesting because I was wondering at times why a girl is never absent from my poetry.

SHIN: The poem, 'All the Garbage of the World, Unite!' from your ninth book, *Your First* (2008), which is also the title of the book in translation, seems to have gotten a lot of attention from readers abroad.

KIM: I was trying to express that perhaps my muse is inside the community of all things discarded after they've been used up. I still remember writing it one afternoon in just one sitting.

SHIN: Two poems, 'Dear Choly, From Melan' and 'Saturn's Sleeping Pill' from your tenth book *Sorrowtoothpaste Mirrorcream* (2011) will be published with this interview, and it appears that the subject matter in both poems is melancholy.

KIM: I was trying to pick relatively easy poems, so I ended up selecting those two about melancholy. And it may also have turned out that way because the whole book is steeped in melancholy.

SHIN: Such melancholy shows up particularly well in 'Manhole Humanity,' but it also seems to organically embody a critical message of civilisation.

KIM: I didn't seek out such subject matter, but rather it just happened organically. I have a tendency to look first and think about the ending of things. This applies to civilisation as well. I frequently imagine civilisation as a makeshift stage or art installation, and a scene in which it all collapses. But lately, I think about living out the rest of my life laughing meaninglessly a rhythmical laugh.

SHIN: I think certain exceptional poets are also exceptional critics. I remember being deeply moved by a piece you wrote on poet Yi Sông-bok. What kind of qualities should one cultivate in order to reach an exceptional level of poetry criticism?

KIM: I think of criticism as something that reads the way thin yet resilient fibrous strings are found inside a sponge gourd after its flesh has been scooped out or something that reads the habitual movement of muscle and bone in the space between the hand and the handle of a broom after sweeping the courtyard of a Buddhist temple a thousand times. Criticism lets you know how a poem has tried to go against the destiny of poetry that is vast yet narrow, and, conversely, it lets you know that the poem has tried so hard to live inside the horizon of such destiny. I like it when a critic's hand enters my poem, touches the bone, then leaves. I like criticism that is written as though it's completing another poem upon meeting a poem in which the critic is also part of the poem. I think everyone knows more or less what the sponge gourd is used for after its flesh has been scooped out, why someone has to sweep the temple's courtyard.

SHIN: Would you choose the life of a poet if you were to be born again?

KIM: I don't want to be born again. I have never thought about being born again as a human who contains 'me'. I have written in a poem that, if I were to be born again, I would be born without any borders, like certain adjectives. And if that is the poetic condition then I have no choice in the matter.

SHIN: For someone who has stepped into your world of poetry for the first time, especially readers abroad, would you please share several key words for your poetry?

KIM: Death, Woman, [South] Korea, You, Seoul, Absence, Illness, Rats, Poetry.

How could I possibly forget this place?

Excerpted from an interview in *Munyejungang* (Summer, 2012) with Kim Hyesoon and poets Yi Ûn-kyu and Kwon Hyôk-ung:

YI: In the poem 'I'm OK, I'm Pig' there are several subtitles such as 'Pig Speaks', 'Pig Pigs Out', 'Your Imperial Majesty, Ferroconcrete!' and 'Kitchen Confidential'. I'm curious if there was a decisive factor that led you to focus on 'Pig' as the primary subject of the poem.

KIM: As you know, last year, three million pigs were buried due to the outbreak of foot-and-mouth disease in our country. And countless numbers of cows were also buried. Almost all of the cows and pigs in South Korea went into the ground. Their pink bodies, whether they were diseased or about to be diseased, were difficult to dispose of, so they were buried alive. I repeatedly watched the scenes of live pigs being dumped by the truckload into a hole as big as a crater lined in plastic. I also watched a documentary made a few years ago by an American. The pigs were covered in their own shit and lived in a tight metal cage just big enough to fit their bodies, unable to lie down or sit. They die within about a year after they are born. Last year, my daughter was at an art residency on the outskirts of the city Goyang, and I occasionally went back and forth to take her some food. During the trip, my car would get sprayed with disinfectant several times. So, whenever I went to that tranquil place, it was as if I'd been to the North Pole. I would stop and wipe off the white disinfectant from my car while looking at the pigsties and cow stalls that had been shutdown. The winter passed and spring came, and I even visited the places the animals had been buried. We handled the pigs not very differently from the way the bodies of the people of this country were handled during the dictatorship. I read *Yamansidae ui kirok* (2006) [The Record of the Barbaric Times – about the history of torture in Korea] all night long, then early in the morning I stuck my head out the balcony door on the 13th floor of my apartment and sang in a screeching pig voice 'How could I possibly forget this place.'* I could only make eye contact with my young students at school after I had cleansed what I had read the night before with a song as pristine as 'Home-sickness.' And, with friends, I went to a Buddhist temple on the east coast to observe a rite to console the souls of all the livestock that had been eaten. But the rite seemed too conventional. I couldn't stand all the colours and the sounds at the temple, so I went to a temple on the south coast. I spent the

---

* 'How could I possibly forget this place?' is from a poem 'Homesickness' (1927) by Chông Chi-yong (1902-50), who was one of the most prominent poets during the Japanese colonial period. According to Kim Hyesoon, everyone in South Korea recognises the phrase because the poem has been turned into a song, which became very popular. [DMC]

night there praying for the livestock that had been killed, but I couldn't meditate. During the meditation I thought of myself, this body of mine that I drag around, this thing made of flesh, blood, its nakedness, an animal that runs full speed ahead towards death, and yet how I was scribbling a poem on a piece of paper trying to become as clear as glass. This poem ['I'm OK, I'm Pig!'] was an attempt at ventilating those pathways with a language that erases things. I live in a world full of death, I head towards death, what is spoken and I are erased simultaneously by silence, and with death-filled language I try to form images – isn't this poetry? Within those hours of meditation, I even thought of my own hands, the hands of a housewife, cooking meat and putting it on the dining table three times a day. I mean, the actions of our language that activate the space of absence, the connection between 'doing' poetry and our daily eating habits.

KWON: If there were such a poem that contains all the poems, this poem might be it. If I were to imitate your poem's wordplay, the pig in your poem is I-Heart-Pig. Adorable I-Love-Pig. Young Pig, God's Pig, carrying all the sins of the world on its back. Borges' Aleph Pig. Multi-dimensional Pig, exposing all the weak in the world in its lone body. How did you obtain Pig's abundance?

KIM: Before the meditation, you are told clichés such as 'mind your body', 'don't get dragged by a Zen koan but pull it along as you go'. Then I start to feel rebellious. At a communion we share Jesus' flesh and blood. During a traditional rite, we share pig's flesh and blood. We are beings that judge and differentiate. We differentiate, yet after we eat and drink, we become one body. Behind Jesus, there is God's love, but what's behind Pig? Like you mentioned, maybe it is best to say that there is Aleph behind Pig. 'To nail Pig on a cross would be too natural,' so what more can I say? There must be Aleph behind all those natural things, the insignificant disposable things, the body. Borges may have looked into a glass bead, but inside it is Pig, the body is locked up inside a tiny sty. As a poet, I can't think that I have touched that, the Aleph.

KWON: Rather than calling it an epic poem, it should be called a narrative poem. Pig is nailed onto a cross – its life journey – gets buried in a hole – conclusion: the poem's steeped in a narrative journey of resurrection. Right now, it makes me think of *The Wasteland* and *Namhae Kûmsan* [by Yi Sông-bok]. Could you briefly say something about the overall structure of the poem?

KIM: During my temple-stay I didn't meditate but followed my delusions instead. After I completed my sham meditation, never mind bowing or practising mindfulness, I went out to the gate of the temple, my head filled with idle thoughts. In my meditation, I was in confusion, swept here there by swarming-pigs-like sensations. One voice dragged in another voice. I may have wished for a polyphony while I wrote.

KWON: It appears that the foot-and-mouth outbreak had a direct effect on the way the poem was conceived. But I also see in the poem glimpses of you as a writer, teacher, a woman poet. There are parts when the inside of Pig and the inside of you the poet are indistinguishably fused, and at times the screams, the humor alone felt like a soliloquy. Weren't you in a lot of pain as you wrote about Pig's death?

KIM: I failed to maintain distance with Pig, so at times I was too close to it as well as too far. I was sad when I was too far, and when I was too close, my body stank.

KWON: I was deeply impressed by your simultaneous wordplays involving humour and sorrow. Pig keeps transforming into: 'a place where there is nothing to eat' (= a place) *in Korean teji [a place] sounds like twaeji [pig]*, '...sounds Pig, pork Pig' (= I've become meat, pork) *in Korean this phrase sounds the same as I'm Pig, meat Pig*, 'Pig pigs out (= dies)' *literal translation is 'Pig dies,' and 'die' [tweji] in Korean also sounds the same as pig [twaeji]*, 'Pig9 (= with a tail coiled around the body),' 'pink Pig.' I tend to believe that, on a deeper level, sense is mutual, that what flows beneath the skin is the same sorrow, laughter. What method do you use to pull out your sensation?

KIM: The language of poetry is a language of absence, so it goes on the path outside of the conventions of language. If you follow the language of poetry, you can hear things even in a death-like space and image patterns emerge. Each blotch of sensation spreads into a different pattern. Then you follow that pattern and another image blooms. There is no particular method to this, but if I had to articulate it, I could say that it is like the way a ghost speaks, the way a subject speaks after its 'me' is erased. So I am not particularly fond of poems in which the 'me' speaks prominently. I dislike hearing a poem even from a poet who evokes immense imagination when 'me' is the one who is speaking. Ultimately, I think the issue is the 'death' of 'me'. If you kill 'me' the contours of sensation get etched automatically. Perhaps I could explain it in this way: that the method involves speaking without speaking. Only then language emerges into silence, to volunteer. Language comes out, dancing. [...]

KWON: I wondered if a poem like 'Bloom, Pig!' was the foundation of your epic poem. Through screams or wails the situation gets aired immediately. I don't know if this expression is appropriate for your piece, but compared to your other work, I think this work is far more direct and visceral. Was this intentional? On one level, without any calculated thought or structure, like a theatre of cruelty, instead of an intellectual reflection on the unbelievable violence in front of you, that the intention was to evoke an immediate response?

KIM: This is the first time I have talked so much about a single poem of mine.

Before I began writing the poem, I kept watching *A Psychological Report on 5.18* Suicides*, a film that was aired in 2009. I still see in my mind those who cannot sleep at all. I watch the scenes of their sleep filmed by an infrared camera. At times, in the middle of the afternoon, I hear their screams when I'm standing under a cherry blossom. Those who have received such harsh treatment [during the Kwangju Massacre] would not be able to see it, but there are moments when I intensely feel a sense of survivor's guilt to the point that my toes curl up. I didn't even get as far as thinking about evoking a response, but while I was writing the poem I wanted the realm of metaphorical sensation to follow after depicting the ways we handle pigs' bodies, which then in turn bring in the sensation of 'Bloom, Pig!'

KWON: I think, through Pig, you are also reflecting on love relations. The ceremony of power relations--to eat or to be eaten, such is the exchange of reciprocity between you and me. Was there any special reason why you depicted love through Pig?

KIM: We say we love each other but we eat each other up. Baudelaire said that even love involves those who are strong and those who are weak. I think of Pig as having the lowest standing within power relations. The body that gets eaten most easily is Pig's. When a love relation changes into a relation of domination, the position of the subjugated plunges further down to Pig's position. Body changes into exchange value. Could you, with that body, oink oink, say, I love you?

[...]

---

* 5.18 refers to the May 18, 1980 Kwangju Massacre or Kwangju Uprising against the military dictatorship in which many students and civilians were killed and injured.

Translator's Note

I met Kim Hyesoon for the first time in Seoul, in 2001. We decided by phone to meet at a Starbucks in an arts district called Hyehwadong, so we could find each other easily. She told me she had glasses and short hair. I did not say I also wore glasses. Somehow it felt important that I find her first the way I had found her poetry while I was searching, actually floundering about, for the right kind of bridge that would allow a return to my first home, South Korea, which I had left in 1972. Kim insisted on treating me to lunch at a noodle shop that she and her husband, the renowned playwright Lee Kang-Baek, often went to. I ordered a hot noodle soup that came with elaborate side dishes. As soon as Kim was done with her simple cold noodles, words began to pour out of her. She began to tell me how she had met her husband soon after the military coup led by General Chun Doo Hwan in 1980. Many consider the 1980s worse than the previous two decades of dictatorship under President Park Chung Hee, a chapter which came to an end with Park's assassination by his intelligence officer in 1979. As soon as General Chun came into power, all publications were even more rigorously censored. Newspapers hit the stands with whole sections blacked out with ink. Kim Hyesoon had just graduated and was working as an editor for a publishing house. She was in charge of Yi's play called *Kaeppul* [Dog's Horns], a piece considered the quintessential expression of life under the military dictatorship of the 1970s. Submitted to state censors, Yi's play came back to Kim completely blackened except for the title and Yi's name. It is from such blackened space that, I believe, Kim Hyesoon's poetry emerges.

Prior to the early 20th century, Korean women's poetry existed primarily within the oral tradition. Women were restricted from learning the written language, which was then classical Chinese, except for Korean script, *hangŭl*, a writing system promulgated in 1446 for women and commoners. The written literary realm was dominated by men and still is. Pioneer women poets of the 1920s published their work publicly for the first time and displayed in their poems acute awareness of Korean patriarchy and oppressive women's conditions. Yet Korean women's poetry since then has been characterised by a language of passivity and contemplation that was predefined by the literary establishment. It wasn't till the late 1970s that a women's poetry energised by feminist consciousness and innovation began to challenge the status quo. And Kim Hyesoon is one of the few women poets, along with Ch'oe Sŭng-ja, to arrive on the scene with a stunning language of resistance to the prescribed literary conventions for women. For Kim the blackened space is the realm in which women from the traditional era expressed their social conditions.

This realm has long been travelled by women represented in Korean shaman narratives, *muga*. In her book of essays called *Yŏsŏngi kŭrŭl ssŭndanŭn kŏtsŭn*

[To Write as a Woman], Kim explores a *muga* called *'Paridegi'* [The Abandoned] also known as *'Parigongju'* [Princess Abandoned] who goes on an arduous journey through the realm of the dead – hell – in search of medicinal water for her ailing parents who had abandoned her at birth for being their seventh daughter – one daughter too many. After saving her parents, *Paridegi* becomes a spirit and guides the dead to another realm. For Kim the blackened space is not only the space of oppression but also a place where a woman redefines herself, retranslates herself. Therefore, I see Kim's poetry as poetry of translation. And in my role as a translator, I guide Kim's translated blackened self to another place, another language, across a bridge forged by history – the history of the US presence in Korea since 1945. The US presence translates into about one hundred US military bases and installations in South Korea, a land that is only one fourth the size of California. Its 1997 economic crisis led to IMF (International Monetary Fund) structural adjustment loans and has made South Korea vulnerable to further control and regulations, the most recent being the Korea-US (KORUS) Free Trade Agreement, which, if enacted, would devastate the already struggling South Korean farmers. Despite South Korea's rise to relative prosperity as the world's eleventh largest economy, the degree to which it remains culturally and politically subservient to the US cannot be underestimated. I need to state the obvious: South Korea is a neocolony.

Kim Hyesoon and I met again, but this time in the US when she was invited to give a reading at Smith College in 2003. We shared a hotel room, and since we thought that there was nothing to do in Northampton, which Kim referred to as 'heaven', we came back to our room. In bed, Kim started to read her poems aloud to me. It struck me that all the poems had rats in them. A few months later, I began translating what I thought of as Kim's 'rat poems', which later Susan Schultz, the editor of *Tinfish*, published as a 'rat chapbook' called *When the Plug Get Unplugged* in 2005. It made total sense to me that Kim's blackened realm would be populated by rats copulating, raising a family, mummy rats gnawing at baby rats, surviving hell. Kim translates hell, as a daughter of a neocolony, and I translate her translated hell as a daughter from the neocolony – two daughters too many. In *To Write as a Woman*, Kim reveals hell as a 'place of death within life...the place Paridegi goes to, the place she travels to via death is a feminine space of creation. It is *hyŏnbin*.' She explains *hyŏn* as 'closed eyes therefore everything is black' and *bin* as 'a signifier for a woman's reproductive organs, a mouth of a lock, a valley, a mountain spring... Inside this dark womb the possibility of all life is held. At that place patriarchy, the male-centred thing breaks, the universality of all things breaks.' Clearly, this is a place of women's chorus, not KORUS.

Kim translates *hyŏnbin*, the blackened realm within the hierarchies of KORUS. Elfriede Jelinek says in her essay, 'Trans - lation (- portation)': 'I gaze into the certain, because the authors I translate knew what makes the clockwork of society tick... And this knowledge about hierarchies and rules drops like a net, like a transparency (transparent!) or banner (bann-her!) over the staged asylum into which we theatregoers are allowed to peer, and which makes it once more into an orderly middle class dwelling, where everything has its place, exactly where it belongs.' Kim's banner acts like a mirror, reflecting back to us the broken hierarchies of KORUS: heavy Fathers, Father's enemy, troops, historical events, and Father's collapsed pink department store and janitors. Kim's rats and dogs roam about Father's broken landscape. Everything breaks and everything gets eaten as 'Seoul eats and shits through the same door' from 'the desire of the abandoned woman wanting to raise an abandoned woman' which Kim says 'leads to the creation of a feminine text. No, it is the text that moves toward desire.' Kim's text is horizontal like the blackened realm towards which *Paridegi* travels. *Paridegi* moves horizontally across space, from life to death. Therefore Kim notes that we see the same things that we see in everyday life in death, as well, including women's daily work. We see mummy washing dishes, making feather breakfasts. And we see a mummy rat and daddy rat and a stranded North Korean submarine that has crossed over to the South and the soldiers who shoot themselves in a suicide pact. Fattened by desire, Kim's rats scurry horizontally in and out of the KORUS of Seoul and chorus of hell. They survive.

Kim Hyesoon and I met once again in 2006 at the American Literary Translators Association's annual conference in Seattle. She was asked by someone what she thought of my translation of her poetry. She answered, 'It is like meeting someone like myself.' Her astute answer implied to me that she thought beyond the well-known and accepted expectation, a faithful or absolute translation, a notion Paul Ricoeur refers to as 'a fantasy of perfect translation'. Instead he argues for the 'loss of linguistic absolute' and proposes the notion of 'linguistic hospitality...the pleasure of dwelling in the other's language is balanced by the pleasure of receiving the foreign word at home, in one's own welcoming house'. Kim understands her translated text as an entirely separate thing, a different house that reminds her of her own house. And because I used to dwell in the same house as Kim, the words or texts that I receive into my new house, distant from the house of my childhood, are not foreign. Therefore, for me 'linguistic hospitality' involves first returning to my childhood home, then departing to my current dwelling in the US. It is an act of linguistic return, and, hence, a perpetual farewell. As in Kim's own translation of the blackened realm where two different realities are accessed from the same horizontal plane, the English translation of Kim's poetry also exists on the same plane as the original poem, but it is made of a different linguistic and cultural mirror. When two such mirrors meet, twoness is forged and become inseparable. My translation is born from the twoness – the chorus of mirrors, mirrors against KORUS.

DON MEE CHOI